LAND OF THE FREE

LAND OF THE FREE
Ulster and the American
Revolution

Ronnie Hanna

Ulster Society (Publications) Ltd. 1992

Published in 1992 by
Ulster Society (Publications) Limited,
Brownlow House, Windsor Avenue,
Lurgan, Co. Armagh BT67 9BJ.

ISBN 1 872076 11 4

COVER ILLUSTRATION: Leslie Stannage.
BACK COVER: The Battle of Yorktown (National Park Service, Yorktown)

For Lorraine and Rachel.

CONTENTS

LIST OF MAPS

ACKNOWLEDGEMENTS

THIS book is the product of the combined efforts of a number of individuals and organisations to whom I am greatly indebted. I would like to pay special thanks to Community Projects Branch of the Training and Employment Agency for their support through the operation of the Ulster Society ACE Scheme. This has provided staff who have been actively involved in the project from its research stage to the final typesetting. One former employee is deserving of a special tribute. Isobel McCulloch carried out painstaking research into the *Belfast News Letter* on my behalf and continued to do so even after the end of her ACE contract. I trust that she will consider the end product worthy of all the time and effort she gave so freely.

Land of the Free has been written at this time to coincide with the special celebrations being held in Larne to mark the 275th anniversary of the sailing of the *Friend's Goodwill* to America in May 1717. The Ulster Society has worked closely with Larne Borough Council to mark this historic event in a meaningful way. This book is but one element in a large programme celebrating the Ulster-American connection. I would like to thank Larne Borough Council for the encouragement and support they have given me in this work.

Finally, I trust that the reader might gain a better understanding and appreciation of the historic link between Ulster and the United States of America from these pages. If that is the case then I will have received my reward.

Ronnie Hanna

... the young men of Ireland who wish to be free and happy should leave it and come here as quickly as possible. There is no place in the world where a man meets so rich a reward for good conduct and industry as in America.

John Dunlap to Robert Rutherford,
letter of 12 May 1785.

Call this war by whatever name you may, only call it not an American rebellion; it is nothing more or less than a Scotch-Irish Presbyterian rebellion.

Unknown Hessian captain (1778), quoted

INTRODUCTION

TO appreciate what America meant to Ulster and what Ulster meant to America in the eighteenth century, one has only to leaf through the pages of the *Belfast News Letter* for those critical years. As well as carrying literally thousands of adverts for the transatlantic passage and the new life beckoning in the "new world", the newspaper also relayed the triumphs and tragedies experienced by relatives and friends who had gone to America.

It is well known that the *Belfast News Letter* was the first journal outside America to carry, in full, the text of the Declaration of Independence, but this was really only the tip of the iceberg. As the years of settlement and struggle turned into years of crisis and conflict, so coverage of American events became more extensive. It was entirely fitting that this should be so for, as will be shown, there were many Ulster actors upon the American stage as the drama of the revolution unfolded.

While this book draws on a number of sources, its bed-rock is the *News Letter*, for in its pages one can experience the immediacy of the events and can begin to understand just how much America's revolution owed to its Ulster heritage.

I

THE ULSTER HOMELAND

AT the beginning of the seventeenth century Ulster was a barren and backward land. Troubled by internecine warfare, the country cried out for peace and progress. The Gaelic chieftains had been defeated by Elizabeth's armies, but what they inherited was little better than a wasteland. The one hope Ulster had was her links with the mainland, especially Scotland; links which went back centuries. That hope now became a reality as the link with Scotland was strengthened and formalised in the shape of the Ulster Plantation. Dr A. T. Q. Stewart has written of this period:

> Immigration from Scotland was fairly continuous for centuries before 1609, and was fact of geography rather than fact of history. What happened in the Stuart reigns was that Scots settlers and entrepreneurs seized an opportunity of renewing a migration, which had been temporarily checked, on very advantageous terms.[1]

Antrim and Down had already experienced Scottish settlements but now thousands more Scots were encouraged to make the short sea journey by the managers of the Crown Plantation. They changed Ulster forever, and they changed with it. Villages and towns were built and the foundations laid for a manufacturing economy. Forests were cleared and marshes drained to develop agriculture. Ulster, which had always been separate from the rest of Ireland, cut off by mountains and swamps, now became as if a different world.

A more fundamental if less obvious change occurred in the character of the country. The Gaelic Irish culture was transplanted by a new and dynamic force which was the culture of the Ulster-British. Stewart again has written on the subject:

> The distinctive Ulster-Scottish culture, isolated from the mainstream of Catholic and Gaelic culture, would appear to have been created not by the specific and artificial plantation of the early seventeenth century, but by the continuous natural influx of Scottish settlers both before and after that episode: in particular, the heavy immigration which took place in the seventeenth century seems to have laid the foundations of the Ulster colony.[2]

The new settlers brought with them a new religion; they were the products of the Reformation. This instilled in them, especially the Lowland Scots, a love of education and learning, a moral regeneration and an appreciation of democratic standards as represented by the Presbyterian Church, rudimentary though that democratic structure may have been. While the Presbyterian faith placed the emphasis on individual salvation and therefore individual effort it was nonetheless a mighty unifying force.

In 1641 that force was put to the test in the Irish Rebellion. The genocidal attack ultimately failed to reverse the Plantation but its impact helped shape the character of the Ulster-British people and steeled them for future trials, particularly at Enniskillen and Londonderry.

The Ulster-Scots proved themselves a resilient people and well qualified for the task of pioneering. They had known hard times in Scotland and now in Ulster they became the backbone of the Plantation. It was almost a natural progression for them to move further west and take on the mantle of builders of the emerging American nation. These were the "Scotch-Irish", a misleading term which should be noted, explained and then dispensed with. Dr James Leyburn, in his seminal work *The Scotch-Irish: A Social History*, provides the explanation:

> The Scotch-Irish, as they came to be known in America, were overwhelming Scottish in ancestry and Presbyterian in faith.[3]

The term and explanation require qualification. If there was one thing the Ulster people were definitely not, it was "Irish". On arriving in Massachusetts in 1718 the Presbyterian Minister Rev.

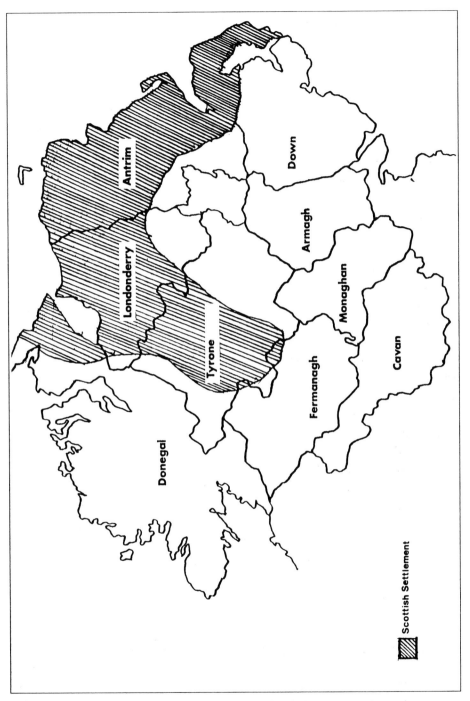

Map 1: *Scottish settlement in Ulster.*

James McGregor, who had been in the Siege of Londonderry, remarked on this misnomer:

> We are surprised to hear ourselves termed Irish people, when we so frequently ventured our all for the British Crown and liberties. We are people of the Scottish race in Ulster who have given our strength and substance and our lives to uphold the British connection there.[4]

If it is wrong to call those who left Ulster for America "Irish" – and it certainly is – then it is almost as inaccurate to term them "Scotch". Although they were conscious of their Scottish background they were of a distinctive character and heritage moulded by the Plantation. The Ulster community that sent so many of its sons and daughters to America in the early eighteenth century had its own identity and they looked to Ulster as their homeland. Dr Leyburn comments:

> In this sense then the Ulstermen of Scottish decent were not truly Ulster-Scots, but people of a new nationality with its own traditions and culture and points of reference . . . What they knew best and loved was northern Ireland.[5]

Leyburn has pin-pointed a number of important differences between the Plantation community and the Scottish motherland. To start with it would be true to say that the Ulster people were not tied to the land to the same extent they had been in Scotland. A greater social and occupational mobility developed in the new land as the opportunity for involvement in business and manufacturing presented itself. This new people became imbued with a desire to better themselves and improve their standard of living. Another change was in the nature of their religion. The Presbyterianism of Ulster was markedly of a less compromising strain than that which developed in Scotland. The emigration to America showed the extent to which the Ulster people were prepared to go in opposing unjust authority and in defence of the principles they believed in. When they were again faced by what they considered tyrannous forces in America they were to the fore in the struggle for liberty.

Apart from the changes that the new land and a new life produced in the Ulster-Scots, perhaps the most clear cut of all the new influencing factors was the dilution of the blood ties with Scotland. The intermixing and intermarriage with the English settlers in the Plantation gave birth to a new people. Theodore Roosevelt has remarked on the character of those who helped build his country:

The Presbyterian Irish were themselves already a mixed people. Though mainly descended from Scotch ancestors, many of them were of English, a few of French Huguenot, and quite a number of true old Milesian Irish extraction. They were a truculent and obstinate people, and gloried in the warlike renown of their forefathers, the men who had followed Cromwell, and who had shared in the defence of Derry and in the victories of the Boyne and Aughrim.[6]

The seventeenth century was a long and hard struggle for the new settlers in Ulster, but by its close they had well and truly established their credentials. By their toils in the fields and the fortified towns and by their courage in the face of terror in the 1640s and 1688-91 they had proven themselves a new force to be reckoned with. Yet for all their sacrifice all they had earned was discrimination and more despair. The land for which they had given so much was now to act as a springboard in the search for freedom and prosperity, which was what had brought them to Ulster in the first place. Their eyes now turned to the west.

As a new century dawned the dissatisfaction of the Ulster people with their lot was very great, because the sacrifices they had made in the previous century had also been very great. The list of grievances was long and it was headed by bitter feeling over the economic conditions they faced. The Ulster people were industrious and ingenious but they were hamstrung by the mercantile system imposed by the British Parliament. The result was that mainland manufacturing and commercial interests had a great advantage over their competitors in Ulster, whose access to British, colonial and foreign markets was limited or denied by statute. When these legal drawbacks were combined with down turns in the economy, as occurred in the linen industry in the 1770s, then the situation was exacerbated and the incentive to look elsewhere for a new start could scarcely have been greater.

If unfair and unjust law was not enough to contend with, the situation was made worse by the greed of the Anglican land-owning class. Tenant farmers were subject to arbitrary rent increases on the expiration of their leases, a phenomenon known as "rack-renting". In many cases tenants had no choice but to give up their farms, often to Gaelic-Irish competitors against whom they had struggled for survival and the preservation of the British connection in recent years. Against this background the American colonies seemed an attractive prospect. In 1719 Archbishop William King wrote about the situation:

> The truth of the case is this: after the Revolution [deposition of James II by William III and Mary, 1688–90] most of the kingdom was waste, and abundance of the people destroyed by the war: the landlords therefore were glad to get tenants at any rate, and set their lands at very easy rents; they invited abundance of people to come over here, especially from Scotland, and they have lived ever since; but now their leases are expired, and they obliged not only to give what was paid before the Revolution, but in most places double and in many places treble, so that it is impossible for people to live or subsist on their farms.[7]

Inevitably those with leases still running now faced the future full of trepidation, and many considered whether it was not better to cut their losses now and join their neighbours in the exodus to a hoped for better life in the New World. A series of bad harvests in the six years between 1714 and 1719 probably helped any waverers make up their minds. Poor rainfall had reduced crop yields and therefore raised food prices. At the same time linen production was depressed, due to the curtailment in the supply of flax. Also in 1716 disease had spread through sheep herds, ruining many farmers. People were suffering great hardship and an indicator was the outbreak of an epidemic of smallpox in 1718 and the prevalence of fever in the community over the next few years. Those who had survived the life or death struggle in the seventeenth century were now dying in the eighteenth century, indirectly at the hands of those for whom they had fought.

Economic hardship was not the only thorn in the side of the Ulster Presbyterians, for in 1704 the passing of the Test Act barred them from all civil and military office under the Crown. All office holders were now required to take the sacrament according to the rights of the Anglican Church. Already Presbyterians had to pay tithes to the Church of Ireland. This uncompromising adherence to a policy of conforming to the Established Church by the Tory government in London demonstrated what was, at best, a lack of appreciation of past sacrifices by the Ulster Presbyterians and, at worst, a deliberate and callous move to mark them as second-class citizens. It is little wonder, then, that the Presbyterians who left Ulster for America carried with them bitter memories of the British government. The Act itself was finally repealed in 1782 and many of those who had suffered under its clauses, no doubt, thought it appropriate that it should disappear at the same time that Britain was forced to recognise the independence of the new American nation, a nation whose rise owed everything to those same Ulster Presbyterians; for now the story switches from the Old to the New World.

II

THE NEW WORLD

CHRISTOPHER Colombus made his voyage of discovery to America in 1492 but it was almost 100 years later that English settlements began to appear on the North American mainland.

In 1585 the colony of Virginia was established by Walter Raleigh. It was not to be a success. The next year Francis Drake brought those colonists still surviving back to England at their request. A fresh attempt to plant the colony in 1587 also foundered. England was now occupied with the threat from Spain but although the colonists disappeared the name of the colony remained, as did English interest. In these early days there were many misconceptions about the potential of North America. Some saw it as a provider of quick and easy profits from mining or because of its supposed position in relation to the mythical North West Passage. A number of economic possibilities were considered, including the production of timber, soap, pitch, wine and olive oil, but it was the availability of land that was the greatest attraction to farmers and farm labourers. There was missionary work to be done as well, while the native Americans and the New World also appealed to the English spirit of adventure. On a more mundane level, the, writer Richard Hakluyt also pointed out that here was a possible solution to the growing problem of vagrancy. Such thinking was well ahead of its time for this would later become official government policy, as employed in relation to the Caribbean and Australia.

Of course there was a very obvious parallel with the Ulster Plantation. In many respects Ulster was seen as a testing ground for a possible colonisation of Virginia. There was another common factor. Both in Ulster and America the colonists or planters were under threat from the natives. During the first nine years of the Virginia Plantation 300 of the settlers returned to England. Ulster faced a similar problem, but here the Scots were ready to take the place of their southern neighbours.

As would be the case in Ulster in the eighteenth century, so early-seventeenth-century England was awash with propaganda calling on discontents to look to the west. Richard Hakluyt was but the greatest of many propagandists for America. The list of benefits was a long one: land was plentiful and labour was in short supply; the rich woodlands offered a limitless trove of fuel and building materials; land was cheap at twelve pounds and ten shillings for 200 acres; and there was no pressure for enclosure of common land in America.

This idyllic view of the New World was a stark contrast to the reality of plague, famine, war and economic depression in England. There was no need for further incentives. A fresh attempt was made to colonise Virginia and this time it succeeded.

On 24 May 1607, 105 settlers arrived at the mouth of the James River in the ships *Susan Constant, Godspeed,* and *Discovery.* They founded the settlement of Jamestown and, despite the problem of having to acclimatise to more extreme temperatures than they had been used to, the colony flourished.

In 1610, Lord De La Warr arrived as Governor with fresh supplies and men. This provided rejuvenation and a new stimulus to the colony just when it was needed.

The source of Virginia's future wealth lay in the production of tobacco, but of course this was not apparent in the early years. Nonetheless, as far as the managers of the Plantation were concerned, there was clearly no future in subsistence farming since this type of life was already available in England. To attract settlers it was necessary to provide a higher standard of living than could be had in Britain. There was some resistance to growing tobacco because of the economic risks associated with concentrating on one staple crop. This would leave the producers at the mercy of the market and smoking was a relatively new phenomenon. Instead, Captain John Smith and his colleagues in the Virginia Company sought to pay for imports by promoting the manufacture of silk, glass, timber, soap, grain and wine. It soon became clear they were swimming against the tide.

John Rolfe was the first of the planters to grow tobacco

commercially, beginning in 1612. There were two main reasons why tobacco should be grown – it was easy and it provided a good profit. Its popularity soon spread with the breaking up of new ground, but in the long run Virginia would pay dear for this development as tobacco growing exhausting the soil after about seven years. There was therefore a steady move westwards in the seventeenth and eighteenth centuries until, by the early 1800s, the state had run out of virgin land for cultivation.

As production rose so prices fell, e.g. 20,000lb was produced in 1619 selling at three shillings per pound, while by 1639 production had risen to 1,500,000lb at 3 pence per pound. The following year the population of the colony reached 10,000 and it was to remain the largest settlement until the revolution.

If Virginia was the source for the emergence of the southern and middle colonies, then the same role was performed in the north by Massachusetts. In 1618 a group of Puritans applied to the Virginia Company for a plantation patent. For a number of reasons the final departure for the New World was delayed for two years, but on 16 September 1620 the famous Pilgrim Fathers set sail from Plymouth aboard the equally famous *Mayflower*. After a troubled voyage the ship arrived in what was to become New England on 9 November. The settlement they founded was also given the name of Plymouth.

It was a harsher region than Virginia in terms of climate and the quality of the soil and this resulted in a slower growth. Between 1630 and 1637 the population rose from 300 to 550 souls, but a firm foothold had nevertheless been made. In 1629 the Massachusetts Bay Company was established and in 1630 John Winthrop arrived to manage its affairs and became the first Governor .

As the 1630s progressed there was a steady flow of Puritan immigrants escaping the economic depression in the cloth trade and the increasing persecution of the nonconformist community by the Archbishop of Canterbury, William Laud. Almost half of the new settlers had been employed in cloth manufacturing and most of them came from East Anglia and the south-west of England.

This Puritan influence, which would soon be matched by the influence of the Ulster Presbyterians further south, left an indelible imprint on the American character. Together the Pilgrims and the Presbyterians were characterised by a spirit of individual struggle and salvation which produced a sober, respectable, decent, self-reliant and energetic people. Hugh Brogan has described this

Top: *The first English settlements in New England
begin to take shape. (Library of Congress)*

Bottom: *The Pilgrim Fathers leave Plymouth.
(Woolara Museum, Bartlesville, Oklahoma)*

development as "the most remarkable work of the English Reformation".

The seeds had now been sown for the growth of a new nation, but in the early years the infant colonies would be most English in character, style and government. If the colonies were ever to become something more than a "greater" Britain then it was clear that something more was needed; a spark to set afire the existing shape of things, remould them and make them as new. That spark came from Ulster and it started in the year 1717.

III

ULSTER SAILS WEST

THERE had already been some Ulster emigration to America before the eighteenth century, but on a small scale. Among the more notable figures to have arrived in the latter part of the seventeenth century were the Presbyterian ministers Samuel Davis, William Trail, Thomas Wilson and Francis Makemie. Makemie was to become the founding father of the Presbyterian Church in America.

Even earlier than this Ulster might have had an impact on the development of the new colonies. However, it was a case of "might have been" for the *Eagle Wing* did not reach its destination in 1636. The vessel had left Groomsport in September carrying 140 passengers who, like the Pilgrim Fathers, were seeking freedom to practice their Protestant faith as they chose. Forced at first to shelter from the storms in Lough Ryan, the *Eagle Wing* was eventually forced to turn back to Ulster after almost foundering in wretched weather off Newfoundland. It was a brave attempt that failed, but in a way it also succeeded for it lit the path for those that were to follow.

Apart from the example of the *Eagle Wing*, which of course was none too auspicious, by the early eighteenth century Ulster people were aware of the success and the potential of the New World, through correspondence from the colonies and the effective propaganda campaign to attract new settlers organised by agents of the shipping companies and the colonies themselves.

The first recorded sailing of an emigrant ship from Ulster to America was that of the *Friend's Goodwill*, which left Larne in April 1717 and arrived in Boston Massachusetts in September. It was to be the first of many.

About 5,000 people left Ulster for America that year to lay the foundations for future immigration and settlement. The letters that came home did not attempt to gloss over the hardships and hazards of a sea journey that could last up to three months in some cases, in cramped and unhygienic conditions, but the message was that it was worth enduring for the rewards waiting in America. The perils of the Atlantic crossing were graphically described in a letter from Samuel McCulloch to his father in Carrickfergus, dated 24 September 1774:

Dear Father
    This comes with our duty to you and our stepmother, and our love to your brothers and sisters, and to let you know that it has pleased God to spare all the principals of our two families, but it was sore on our children; for on the 19th June, Tommy Jackson died, and the day after the two girls, to our great grief, both died in one hour. This was the greatest trouble I ever felt, to see our two fine girls thrown into the ocean after they had been seven weeks on board and were on the coast. Our mate died, and several more men and women and about 12 children. We had a great fever on board; men lay raving through all the berths. I never lay down that night, but I was afraid that some of us would have it before the morning. Our children died of a short illness and not of the fever.
    When we came to York, Billy and me went onshore, and at about 3 o'clock we set out for our brother's but we could not come to his house, and we lay down and slept in a wood.[1]

Most of these early settlers came to Pennsylvania where there was an abundance of cheap, fertile land and where the authorities were helpful. The following year several thousand more followed the vanguard and the impact of Ulster began to be felt. Many of those who left Ulster were ministers of the Presbyterian Church, as W. F. Marshall has highlighted:

The Rev. William Boyd of Macosquin, and the Rev. William Cornwall of Clogher, came with the emigrants of 1718. In the same year there went out, amongst others, the Rev. William Elliot, the Rev. James Woodside, the Rev. James McGregor, and the Rev. William Tennent. In the following year came the Rev. James Hillhouse and the Rev. Samuel Young with two licentiates, John

McKinstry and Samuel Dorrance, to be followed in succeeding years by a great army of ministers, licentiates and students who built up the Presbyterian Church of North America on the foundation laid previously by Makemie of Ramelton, and firmly planted its Blue Banner across the sea. Most notable, however, was the Rev. James McGregor, of Aghadowey, who was accompanied by a large section of his congregation. These emigrants of 1718 founded and settled the township of New Londonderry in New Hampshire. They settled also at Worcester, and in a short time they founded numerous settlements in New Hampshire and Maine.[2]

Marshall goes on to say about the town:

For it was not for nothing that the new township was called Londonderry. Many of the settlers were veterans of the famous siege, and that siege was one of their proudest memories. It is recorded that the song most frequently sung round their firesides was the ballad of the Boyne Water. Oldish men who had starved and fought on Derry Walls, and youngish men reared in the Derry tradition were not men to be trifled with.[3]

For a few years after the initial influx of Ulster settlers in 1717 and 1718 there was a slackening off in numbers, but in 1725 the migration received a fresh impetus. For the next four years the down-turn in the economy encouraged many Ulster families to pull up their roots and follow in the wake of their fellow countrymen and women who had already undertaken the great adventure. They left in such numbers that it was remarked upon in Parliamentary circles and the private correspondence of the great and the good. The Archbishop of Armagh, Hugh Boulter, remarked in a letter of 16 July 1728:

We have hundreds of families (all Protestants) removing out of the North to America; and the least obstruction in the linen manufacture, by which the North subsists, must occasion the greater number following . . .[4]

The 1730s were comparatively quiet but in 1740 an outbreak of famine, which was to claim 400,000 lives across Ireland, sparked off a third wave of emigration. The Ulster settlement now began to spread outside Pennsylvania along the Great Valley and the Shenandoah Valley into North and South Carolina. Bad harvests in Ulster brought more settlers to these areas in 1754 and 1755, but the outbreak of war with the French and the Indians at the same time stemmed this flood of immigration before it could reach its peak.

With the return of peace came more new settlers from Ulster. From 1771 to the outbreak of hostilities with Britain in 1775 was the period when emigration from Ulster was at its height. Between 25,000 and 30,000 entered the American colonies, forced out of their homeland by depression in the linen industry and persecution on the tenant farms. The great increase in rents on the Antrim estates of the Marquis of Donegall was particularly devastating. In many cases the only alternative to emigration appeared to be destruction.

This then was the greatest exodus of Ulster Protestants in the eighteenth century and it was also to be the last as relations between the American colonies and Great Britain deteriorated to the point of war.

For those who did make the break from the Old World there was a price to be paid, but they knew it was worth paying. Almost one in three of the Ulster Presbyterians who sailed to America did so under contracts of service or indenture, as it was then termed. Contracts for terms of between four and seven years were most common and reflected the great need in the colonies for hired help. The *Belfast News Letter* carried many adverts for passage to America, most of which made special provision for contracted labour. An example was the following advert which appeared on 29 June 1750:

> That the Snow HAWKE, Captain Brown, lately advertised in this paper, will certainly sail from the Lough of Belfast, on the 8th July next, for Newcastle in America, and as the owners are resolved to take in no other goods than provisions for the passengers, any who are not contracted are desired to apply immediately to William Walton and Hugh Pringle of Belfast, Merchants, otherwise they will be disappointed as the number they design to take is near completed. NB Servants will meet with proper encouragement.[5]

Also on 6 June 1752 the paper carried this advert:

> The Good Ship HOLDERNESS, Captain William Simpson Commander, Burthen 300 tons, a new Vessel belonging to Captain

William Blair of Philadelphia is now lying in the Harbour at Larne and will be ready to sail for the said place by the 10th June next. Such as determine to take their passage on her, or any that incline to go as Servants on Redemption, may expect to meet with as good usage as those who have hitherto sailed with Mr Blair who is well known to the county in this Trade. Application may be made to Mr James Bragels in Belfast and James Blair, son of the said William Blair, in Larne or to the Captain on board, who will treat on the easiest terms. Dated May 22nd 1752.[6]

Newcastle and Philadelphia were the destinations for the following sailing, advertised on 21 April 1767:

For NEWCASTLE AND PHILADELPHIA.
The Ship NEWRY PACKET Seymour Hood Master, full 300 tons burthen, just off the stocks, extremely well found and a prime sailer, will be ready to sail for said ports by the 25th May next from Newry. Passengers, redemptioners or servants may expect the best treatment and as the ship is more than half freighted with dairy goods, no greater number than 70 or 80 passengers will be accepted. Those who therefore intend to embrace this favourable opportunity are requested to make immediate application to Hamilton Pringle at Caledon, Mr John Dickson of Newry, Merchant, or any of the passengers who came over in the said ship from Philadelphia. Any that reside at or near Stewartstown or Charlemont may apply to George Hannyngton of Dungannon, Esq;
Newry 20th April 1767.[7]

It was indeed ironic that many of those seeking freedom in America could only hope to achieve it by becoming servants, but it was very much a case of things getting worse before they got better. As well as providing free passage to America the contracts of indenture generally offered fair terms, usually guaranteeing those involved specific points of assistance after the completion of their contract. The best terms available seemed to be those in Pennsylvania where, after service had been completed, the former servant was granted fifty acres of land, an axe, two hoes and two suits of clothing. It was little wonder then that Pennsylvania became Ulster's gateway to the New World.
The main ports to handle this mass of humanity leaving Ulster

were Belfast, Londonderry, Larne, Newry, and Portrush. Once the Atlantic had been safely crossed the vessels would arrive at Philadelphia or Chester or New Castle. By 1729 it was reported that there was already 6,000 Ulster settlers in the colony and this trend would continue right up to the outbreak of the Revolution. This was indeed the best place for the Ulster people to come for in truth they were not particularly welcome in the Puritan community of New England, while the plantation systems of the southern colonies was a completely alien environment. In particular the south-eastern area of Pennsylvania offered a fertile soil a good climate a fair system of government and religious toleration. It reflected well on the foundations laid by William Penn.

Pennsylvania was then the cradle of the Ulster-America community, and in particular its chief port and town, Philadelphia. In a way this town represented the hope which attracted so many Ulster settlers to America. By the time the Ulster immigrants began to arrive in great numbers Philadelphia had already established itself as the chief trading rival to Boston. By 1760 it had become the largest city in the American colonies, with a population of 23,750. During the next 15 years, thanks in large part to the numbers leaving Ulster, this figure almost doubled to around 40,000 at the outbreak of the War of Independence.

It was easy for the Ulster settlers to retain a sense of identity as they tended to settle together and mix little with the English and Germans already there. Another factor was that poverty forced many away from the more expensive land in the east to the frontier regions. Here land was available cheap or often for free as many simply squatted in defiance of the authorities. There were drawbacks, however, especially exposure to attack by the Indians. In this respect colonial officials were glad to have the Ulster people where they were, as they provided a buffer against the hostile natives. When trouble did arise these Ulster settlers were left to their fate; an experience which hardened and embittered them against their government, just as had been the case in Ulster.

From Pennsylvania the Ulster settlement spread along the Valley of Virginia during the 1730s and '40s, following the Great Philadelphia Wagon Road. This was the famous "back country" where their presence was welcomed as a reinforcement against the Indian threat. It was this threat that kept some of the Ulster families moving into the sparsely populated upland regions of North and

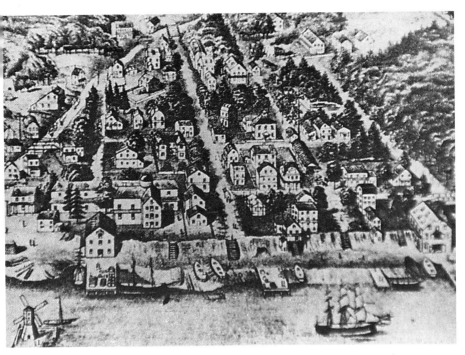

A panoramic view of Philadelphia. (New York Public Library)

South Carolina. Again they were encouraged to do so by the authorities and by force of economic circumstance, reflecting the growing pressure for land in Pennsylvania. Most of the movement into North Carolina took place between 1740 and 1756 with the surge into South Carolina developing in the 1760s. By the time war came with Britain about 90 per cent of the Ulster settlers had made their homes in Pennsylvania, the Valley of Virginia and the Carolinas.

Before war with Britain, however, came war with the Indians. In British history it is known as the Seven Years War, a battle for empire against the French, lasting from 1756 to 1763. William Pitt the elder had become the King's first minister with a determination to crush the French as Britain's last economic and military rival. He felt that it was a war that would pay for itself from the economic prizes on offer, and indeed the size of the British Empire was doubled with the capture of the French Sugar Islands, Canada, India, and Florida. The Ulster community in the American "back country", however, had quite a different perspective on these events. Fighting with France's Indian allies broke out in 1754 and was marked by great cruelty and ruthlessness on both sides. While Pitt was directing British forces towards imperial glory, the Ulstermen were fighting for their survival against an enemy seeking to recover the land he had once occupied. This life or death struggle continued for a year after Britain and France had concluded peace in the Treaty of Paris. Pontiac's War, from 1763–64, gave renewed impetus to the Indian onslaught on the white settlements. Sporadic warfare between settler and native remained a feature of frontier life as this report in the *Belfast News Letter* of 20 February 1767 shows:

> Letters from Fort Prince George, Keowee, say that on the 9th of last month seven traders from Virginia who were carrying goods into the Cherokee country, were found murdered near Cowee. Those traders had sent notice of their approach and a party ... was immediately sent to escort them in found their dead bodies. The goods were not touched, only some paint is said to be missing. The murder is thought to have been committed by some Cherokees in revenge for the people they lost in Virginia about two years ago.[8]

The Ulster settlers emerged from this baptism of fire perhaps a more formidable force than they had ever been. Abandoned to their fate by their British masters, who had let them down so many times in the past, the Ulstermen and women began to feel themselves American above everything else. They had every right to, for it was the future of America that they were working and fighting for.

The division between the frontier community and the old settlements, which was later to become the division between west and east or "country boy" and "city slicker", in its embryonic stage was an Ulster-American phenomenon. It was from this starting point that the Ulster families would be in the vanguard of the push west. Moving across the mountain barriers, many would leave Virginia for Kentucky or North Carolina for Tennessee, while many migrated from eastern Pennsylvania into the Ohio Valley. Theodore Roosevelt pays tribute to this later remarkable chapter in the history of the Ulster-Americans:

> The backwoodsmen were Americans by birth and parentage, and of mixed race; but the dominant strain in their blood was that of the

Presbyterian Irish – the Scotch-Irish as they were often called. These Irish representatives of the Covenanters were in the west almost what the Puritans were in the northeast, and more than the Cavaliers were in the south. Mingled with the descendants of many other races, they nevertheless formed the kernel of the distinctively and intensely American stock who were the pioneers of our people in their march westward, the vanguard of the army of fighting settlers, who with axe and rifle won their way from the Alleghanies to the Rio Grande and the Pacific.[9]

The Ulster Presbyterians were not exclusively confined to the frontier and the areas already mentioned. Smaller pockets of settlement did exist elsewhere. The colonies of New York and New Jersey received a smaller number of Ulster settlers, as the demands there for indentured labour were not as great as those of the colonies to the south. Delaware also had some Ulster settlement, due mainly to the fact that the port of New Castle received many of the immigrants. The potential for settlement here was limited by the fact that the colony was already well populated. The main area of settlement was in the north-east in Cecil County, but after completing their contracts of service most of the Ulster settlers then moved to the open spaces of Virginia and North Carolina.

Further south, the coastal region of South Carolina also acted as a starting point for Ulster settlement. As in Maryland, the few Ulster families that stayed here mostly did so only until their term of indenture ended. The plantation system and the dominant position of the Anglican church in this region was not to the taste of the Ulster settlers and it was to the west that they turned their eyes. Similarly the Puritanism of New England was not accommodating to the Ulster emigrants, although the area did receive about 20,000 of these settlers, as reflected in the place-names across the country. The names of their homeland was something the Ulster people carried with them across all of America, as Marshall has noted in some detail:

There are eighteen towns in the United States named after Belfast. There are seven Derrys, nine Antrims and sixteen Tyrones. There is a Coleraine in Massachusetts. New Hampshire has Stewartstown. Washington, Ohio and Iowa have each a Pomeroy. Hillsborough is in New Hampshire, Illinois, North Dakota and Wisconsin. Maine has Newry. Ohio has Banbridge. In twelve States there are twelve Milfords. In Michigan there is a town named after that river that is not in Ulster, but was once dyed red with Ulster blood, the famous River Boyne.[10]

As well as the familiar names from home the Ulster settlers also transplanted their church to the new world. W. F. Marshall claims that by 1760 America had over 300 Presbyterian congregations (in 1705 there had been only seven) and that during the period between 1680–1820 almost 300 ministers of Ulster descent served in the American Presbyterian Church.

There had been a small Presbyterian presence in the American colonies before 1717 but, with the arrival of the Ulster settlers, Presbyterianism quickly out-stripped the Congregationalists and the Quakers as the main crusading force on the continent. It was no coincidence that the revival known as the "Great Awakening" occurred in the 1730s as Ulster immigration increased. The "Great Awakening" was the American counterpart to the birth of Methodism. It was a time of great change in spiritual affairs but many were repelled by the hysteria associated with the revival. One of the consequences was therefore a division within the Protestant faith in America between the followers of the "New Light", who were caught up in the spirit of the "Great Awakening", and the followers of what was known as the "Old Light", who adhered to longer-established and quieter forms of religious practice. It was also a split between the liberal and rational religion of the urban areas and the fundamentalist faith of the frontier, which of course was where the Ulster settlers were to be found.

If the Ulstermen and women were natural frontiersmen it was also true to say that the frontier helped shaped their character into something new, and something that we now recognise as American. The distances between homes on the American frontier was in contrast to the village pattern of settlement in Ulster and resulted in fostering a greater sense of individuality and independence than had been the case in the Old World. A life of continual movement to new grounds broke down social barriers and put the onus on individual achievement.

Since these Ulster settlers helped make the land they lived in it was not long before they came to regard themselves as American, rather than as an immigrant community. As Britain and the

American colonies began to grow further apart, the opportunity would soon be at hand for these sons and daughters of Ulster to make good their claim to nationhood and to be a new people. Theodore Roosevelt's pen sweeps majestically across the magnificent story of the Ulster-American people, from their arrival in the early eighteenth century up to this point when the fight for freedom beckoned:

They did not begin to come to America in any numbers till after the opening of the eighteenth century; by 1730 they were fairly swarming across the ocean, for the most part in two streams, the larger going to the port of Philadelphia, the smaller to the port of Charlestown. Pushing through the long settled lowlands of the seacoast, they at once made their abode at the foot of the mountains, and became the outposts of civilization. From Pennsylvania, whither the great majority had come, they drifted south along the foothills and down the long valleys, till they met their brethren from Charlestown who had pushed up into the Carolina back-country. In this land of hills, covered by unbroken forest, they took root and flourished, stretching in a broad belt from north to south, a shield of sinewy men thrust in between the people of the seaboard and the red warriors of the wilderness. All through this region they were alike; they had as little kinship with the Cavalier as with the Quaker; the west was won by those who have been rightly called the Roundheads of the south, the same men who, before any others, declared for American independence.[11]

IV

CROWN AND COLONY

IN coming to America, the Ulster settlers were moving from one colonial situation to another. The harsh experiences of life in Ulster were to be repeated here, albeit in a different form. What did not change however, and was of critical importance in the history of the Ulster-Americans, was the fact that in the New World, as in the Old, they were to experience disillusion and disaffection from the legal authorities.

There was already an undercurrent of discontent in the American colonies with British rule, but as the Ulster influence began to grow so this undercurrent swelled into a rising tide that would sweep away all the edifices of British power. On reflection there is something inevitable about the movement of the Ulster people to finally stake their claim for independence in America's soil, but it would also be true to say that their English rulers brought much of these troubles on themselves.

If one has to single out a year when this course was set, definitely and irreversibly, it was 1763. In that year Britain successfully concluded her Seven Years War against France, and Grenville succeeded Lord Bute as Prime Minister. The two events were related. Although France and her Indian allies had been defeated, the war had been a costly one in America and it still had to be paid for. Grenville came to office with a determination to impose economies on government spending and spread the burden of imperial defence which he considered inequitable. In the case of the American colonies this meant that the onus lay with the colonists themselves to pay for British army protection. Pontiac's rising and the French threat demonstrated the vulnerability of the American colonies and their reliance on the army. It was also accepted that

British troops were needed on a regular basis to deter smugglers and to keep the peace among the more boisterous elements of the fur trade. In the opinion of the British commander in North America, General Amherst, permanent garrisons were needed in Newfoundland, Cape Breton, Prince Edward Island, Nova Scotia and Florida.

When Grenville did his sums he found that the exchequer needed to set aside £372,774 each year to protect Gibraltar, Minorca and the American colonies, the latter claiming the lion's share of the budget. The new prime minister felt it was unfair to ask British landowners to pay for American defence, but he was also convinced that it was impracticable to do so. The idea of increasing taxation at home was one that could not be seriously considered, having witnessed the public unrest in the West Country when Bute had attempted to introduce an excise tax on cider earlier that year. People felt that they had already suffered enough deprivation during the war.

If Grenville needed any further reason to justify a decision to tax the colonies then it was provided by the argument that America was guilty of biting the hand that fed it. Not only had the colonies been reluctant to raise revenue for the war effort (Massachusetts only agreed after Pitt had promised that the colony would be reimbursed after the war), but it was also felt that American trade with France had actually strengthened Britain's enemy. This was certainly the opinion of Pitt, who was by no means anti-American in his general views. Grenville was therefore convinced that taxation of the America colonies was just, necessary and deserved.

Grenville took the initiative in 1764 with the introduction of the Sugar Act which was calculated to raise £45,000 per annum. This was followed in 1765 by the Stamp Act which now required all legal documents (wills, conveyances etc) to carry a government stamp. The tax was already in operation in Britain and it was now to be extended to the American colonies. The initial American response was to look for other means of raising revenue but Grenville was not interested. There was to be no compromise on the principle that Parliament had the right to tax the colonies.

Although the measure went further than many expected, to cover items such as liquor licences, mortgages, insurances policies, pamphlets and newspapers, it was by no means a severe financial burden on the colonists. That fact, however, was almost irrelevant. If Grenville felt he was standing on a point of principle then so too did the colonists. They were equally adamant that there could be no compromise on the issue of no taxation without representation. Unlike the Sugar Act, which was concerned with imperial trade, the Stamp Act was a direct tax: as such it was the exclusive prerogative of the colonial assembles to introduce such a measure.

The Stamp Act also had serious implications beyond its immediate effect. There was now a growing apprehension that this was but the first step in a plan to shift the entire financial burden of administering the empire from the mother county to the colonies, while at the same time the crown would begin to exercise greater authority at the expense of the colonial assembles. A clear rift now began to emerge between Britain and America.

The opposition to the Stamp Act in fact was the culmination of a steadily growing series of grievances with British rule. One particular thorn in the flesh was the dispute over the appointment of judges. This was the exclusive privilege of the crown but colonial opinion, especially in New York, New Jersey and Pennsylvania, was in favour of security of tenure for judges during good behaviour. This had been the practice in Britain since 1701 but the imperial power was reluctant to grant a similar right to the colonies, fearing that judges would show too much favour to the colonies if their position depended on the will of the assembles.

Almost inevitably religion was also a source of conflict. The long-standing primacy of the dissenting faith was now being challenged by the growing influence of Anglicanism. The Archbishop of Canterbury, Thomas Secker, who was appointed in 1758, was instrumental in the opening of the Anglican missionary church in Cambridge, Massachusetts. Pressure was put on the British government to veto the Massachusetts Act which had established the Congregational missionary society to work among the Indians and a campaign was started calling for the appointment of bishops in the colonies. The idea of being ruled by bishops was one that did not lend itself well to Ulster Presbyterians or English Puritans. American opposition to the introduction of bishops was reported in the *Belfast News Letter* of 24 September 1771, the report having been filed on 15 June in Williamsburg, Virginia:

The General Assembly for this province came to the following Resolution on Friday last.

Resolved, *nemine contradicente*, that the thanks of this House be given to the Rev Mr. Henly, the Rev Mr. Gwatkin, the Rev Mr Hewit and the Rev Mr Bland, for the wise and well timed opposition they have made to the pernicious project of a few mistaken Clergymen for introducing an American Bishop, a measure by which much disturbance, great anxiety and apprehensions, would certainly take place among his Majesty's faithful American subjects;. And that Mr Richard-Henry Lee and Mr Bland do acquaint them therewith. By the House of Burgesses G Wythe C.H.B.[1]

Reports in the *News Letter* demonstrate how closely the ideal of American liberty was linked to the Protestant faith, again reflecting the Ulster influence. The edition of 20–24 January 1775 contains the text of an appeal to the people of Massachusetts Bay. It was signed by John Hancock on behalf of the Provincial Congress and contained this significant passage:

> ... the general tenor of our intelligence from Great Britain, with the frequent reinforcements of the army and navy at Boston, excites the strongest jealousy that the system of Colony Administration, so unfriendly to the Protestant Religion, and destructive of American liberty, is still to be pursued, and attempted with force to be carried into execution.[2]

The American colonists also challenged British opinion and policy on military matters. While the British army felt it was shouldering a disproportionate part of the burden of defending the colonies, the men and women on the frontier had quite a different perspective. The colonists argued that they had played a significant part in all Britain's military successes in North America, such as the capture of Louisbourg on Cape Breton Island. In contrast, General Braddock had led his army to disaster on the Pennsylvania frontier in 1765 and General Amherst had helped provoke Pontiac's uprising by underestimating the capabilities of the Indians. The colonists could also argue, with some justification, that the army which finally defeated the French was mainly enlisted in America and employed locally-learned tactics for the warfare in the woods. In fact, the key to the military question was co-operation: the Americans providing troops, tactics, supplies and some funds and the British providing organisation, training, discipline some supplies and most of the funds.

A Boston demonstration against the Stamp Act. (Library of Congress)

Linked to the problem of defence was the question of relations with the Indians. Broadly speaking the British approach was conciliatory, so that intermittent costly war might be avoided. The British government wanted agreements with the Indians to be honoured, and fair compensation paid for land taken. In 1763, a Royal proclamation limited the western expansion of colonial territory. The aim was to direct new settlement into the underpopulated colonies of Nova Scotia, Georgia, West Florida and East Florida. The new settlers, and in particular the Ulster frontier community, would have none of it. Having been forced to quit their homeland by what they regarded as an ungrateful and unjust government, they were not now about to surrender the freedom to live where they wished, a freedom they cherished dearly, to that same government. The Ulster pioneers simply disregarded the King's writ and continued to push westward.

In America, a new and radical leadership began to come to the fore in politics. In a short time it would completely overwhelm the moderate and conservative leadership which had so far ruled the colonies. In Virginia, Patrick Henry and a number of others carried through a number of anti-Stamp Act resolutions embodying the central principle of no taxation without representation. In Massachusetts, the General Court proposed that delegates from all the colonies should meet to co-ordinate opposition to the Stamp Act. It was also in Massachusetts that political protest first spilled over into civil disturbance. A crowd destroyed one of the houses of the newly appointed Distributor of Stamps for Massachusetts, Andrew Oliver, and burned an effigy of the unfortunate man. Oliver was probably relieved that it was only an effigy that went up in flames and resigned his office the next day. Twelve days later, the mob attacked the Vice-Admiralty Court and the houses of the Registrar of the Court, the Comptroller of Customs and the home of Chief Justice Hutchinson. Although there was more to these riots than simple anti-British protest the imperial authorities were rightly worried by the precedent that had been set. Such fears proved well-founded as the example of the Boston riots was quickly taken up elsewhere. The usual practice was to burn effigies of the local stamp distributors with a book tied to the shoulder (representing Lord Bute!), pull down the houses of the leading crown officials and generally terrorise the same.

On 7 October 1765, the appeal of the General Court of

Massachusetts for a meeting of colonial delegates bore fruit with the convening of what became known as the Stamp Act Congress. It was a significant title and a historic event, although only nine of the thirteen colonies were represented. In total there were 27 delegates present from Massachusetts, Rhode Island, Connecticut, Pennsylvania, Maryland, South Carolina, New York, New Jersey and Delaware. Three main policy proposals where discussed covering the prevention of the use of the stamps, the severance of trade with Britain and the possibility of continuing trade without complying with the Stamp Act regulations. In all its debates and discussions the Congress displayed a remarkable degree of unity. For perhaps the first time a feeling of being American could be identified. This was the most significant outcome of the meeting as the Stamp Act was already effectively null and void. In fact, Georgia was soon the only colony where stamps were distributed and that was not to last much longer. The American colonies had demonstrated that when pressed they were a force to be reckoned with, both in the shape of their public representatives and also vigilante groups like the Sons of Liberty.

In 1766, Lord Rockingham succeeded Grenville as prime minister and the new administration immediately moved to repeal the Stamp Act. The new government was clearly more sympathetic to the colonies than its predecessor, and as such it was severely criticised in the House of Commons for giving in to the colonies which some argued would lead only to further demands and further concessions, with the ultimate result being independence. To quell this protest, Rockingham's government introduced the Declaratory Act which asserted the right of parliament to order colonial affairs. This was more than merely a sop to the government's critics as some considered it an essential measure in order to ensure the repeal of the Stamp Act. However, the contrast between the debates in Parliament and in the Stamp Act Congress were the first sign of an irreversible change in the relationship between Britain and the American colonies. While the British ruling class could not countenance or even contemplate any degree of independent authority for the colonists, the Americans quite clearly were no longer prepared to sit quietly and accept the direction of what they increasingly considered was a remote, unfair and incompetent government. While the repeal of the Stamp Act was celebrated in the American colonies with expressions of loyalty, it was a loyalty that now had qualifications firmly attached to it. In 1767, the spectre of conflict re-emerged when the Chancellor of the Exchequer, Charles Townsend, proposed that the American colonies be taxed in order to help reduce the national debt. Although the motion was defeated, the situation was exacerbated when the Grenville opposition depleted government revenues by carrying a motion which reduced land tax by a shilling in the pound. Townsend now felt justified in seeking to raise revenue from the American colonies and he was confident that he could do so without provoking protest.

The chief instrument Townsend intended to use was the Revenue Act which introduced duties on glass, lead, paper and tea and to assist in the collection of these new taxes an American Board of Customs Commissioners was established. The following year, 1768, four new Vice-Admiralty districts were created in Halifax, Boston, Philadelphia and Charles Town with the aim of making the customs and law-enforcement systems more water-tight. The fact that trials would be conducted without juries was seen by many Americans as an attack on fundamental civil rights and they were further outraged when a colonial list was drawn up, using money raised by the new duties, to pay the salaries of imperial officials, e.g. governors, customs officers, etc. From the view-point of the colonies, not only were they now being taxed unfairly, but the democratic structure that existed within the framework of the colonial assemblies was being subverted by the British Crown and Parliament, whose officers were no longer answerable to the local community.

In total, Townsend's policy was a deliberate attempt to centralise power in Britain. This was offensive in the extreme to colonies which had grown accustomed to effective self-government. In all the colonies the elected lower house had gained ascendancy over the upper house (the council) and the executive (the governor). In Virginia, the House of Burgesses governed the colony along the lines of the nineteenth-century British parliament, with the great plantation owners the dominant group. Further north, it was the merchant class that effectively controlled the assemblies, while in Pennsylvania the Quakers still held sway. The British were not then dealing with a mere rabble, although some members of parliament did delude themselves that this was the case. The opposition to Townsend's policies soon became more widespread, varied and

John Hancock. (Museum of Fine Arts, Boston)

prolonged than that to the Stamp Act, reflecting a better organised campaign by the patriot leaders. Sam Adams of Massachusetts was able to rally a formidable movement against British policy and the fear that the next step would be the introduction of bishops and the use of colonial revenue to support a standing British army.

Developments in America were matched by a hardening of attitudes in London. George III was totally opposed to any compromise with the colonists and most members of parliament seemed to be prepared to follow the King's lead. Lord Hillsborough, the first holder of the office of Secretary for the American colonies, now instructed the governors to dissolve all the colonial assemblies. The last to do so was New York in 1769. In Boston, the American patriots responded by harassing customs officials and on 10 June 1768, major riots broke out after the seizure of John Hancock's ship, *Liberty*, on suspicion of smuggling Madeira. Hancock, whose forebears came from County Down, was destined to become one of the leading actors in the great drama that was about to unfold, but for now, all eyes were on Britain's response. Two regiments were quickly dispatched to maintain order, demonstrating that the emphasis of government policy was very much on retaining control of the inhabitants rather that defending the western frontier. Sam Adams now organised a convention in Boston, which in effect was an unofficial meeting of the House of Representatives which had been prorogued by Governor Bernard. Although the conservative element was strong enough to prevent the adoption of any really radical measures, events in Boston were an inspiration to the embryo patriot and non-importation movement developing in other colonies such as New York, Pennsylvania, South Carolina and Virginia, where a certain ex-militia colonel by the name of George Washington persuaded the assembly to boycott British produce. Support for the non-importation movement was especially strong in areas of Ulster settlement. Henry Steele Commager refers to the situation in New York:

> ... only a few hundred men in Orange and Ulster counties, a region of mainly freehold farms, refused to sign the Association to boycott British goods in 1775, while about 3,500 signed.[3]

An indication of the growing tension was the following report in the *Belfast News Letter* of 30 January 1770:

London – Measures that are resolved with regard to North America have now transpired. A squadron of men of war is ordered to be fitted out on board of which four Regiments are to embark, with a proportionate train of artillery; and if the Provinces do not submit to legal measures, without opposition, they will be taught that obedience which is due from colonies to the legislature of their Mother country.[4]

Across the Atlantic, the actions of Massachusetts were condemned by Lord Hillsborough, but by 1769 all the American colonies, with the exception of New Hampshire, were refusing to import British goods. Crown and colony were now on a collision course and it was once again Boston that was the focal point. Both sides were nervous and were guilty of excesses. On 22 February 1770, an eleven-year-old boy was shot dead by another citizen during a bout of rioting, but more serious events were to come. On 5 March, five colonists were shot dead by troops during an attack on the Customs House. "The Boston massacre" seemed to confirm the worst fears about British intentions and New Hampshire now stepped into line with the rest of the colonies. The *News Letter* of 6 July 1770, highlighted the prominent role played by John Hancock in the developing trade-war in Britain. Arguing in favour of turning away British cargo vessels, Hancock addressed an opposition rally in Boston in April:

If a vessel with the plague on board, were coming in here we surely have an undoubted right to fend her off; no person will deny this; why then have we not the same right to send back these goods, which are worse than the plague? The plague might only cause the death of hundreds of thousands; the goods would occasion the ruin of the country, and bring slavery on millions yet unborn.[5]

The *News Letter* further reported on the development of colonial opposition on the 7 August 1770:

that the resolutions at New York for importation were received both at Philadelphia and Boston with the utmost indignation. The inhabitants of Maryland, Pennsylvania, New Connecticut, Boston and Salem, have excluded the people of Rhode Island from trading with them and they have sent back their vessels till they shall fully come into the non importation agreement subsisting in the other colonies and have made satisfaction for their late scandalous defection; so that all hopes of trade this year to the colonies are over.[6]

However, just as events appeared to be reaching a head, the situation was defused by the news that the Townsend duties had been repealed. New York, Philadelphia and Boston quickly resumed trade with Britain but, while calm was restored, there was every likelihood that the storms would return.

If there was to be trouble again then it was most likely that it would be among the Ulster settlers who had already marked themselves as patriots in a new cause. In Pennsylvania, the Ulster men and women had raised a voice of protest against the abandonment of the frontier settlements to Indian attack and against the domination of the assembly by the eastern region. This struggle between west and east coalesced into what became know as the Regulation movement in South and North Carolina. It was largely an Ulster-Scots phenomenon. In South Carolina, between 1766 and 1772, the Regulators pressed for the extension of government and the court system to the back country which had been neglected and was exploited by bandits.

In North Carolina, the movement peaked between the years 1768 and 1771, when the Ulster settlers protested against exorbitant taxation, unfair representation in the legislature and against discriminatory laws imposed on them. The *Belfast News Letter* gave extensive coverage to reports of the regulation movement. On 20 August 1771, a report listed some of the grievances of the Ulster-American community in North Carolina, concluding a determined challenge to the Governor:

They were determined to contend unwearied for their constitutional rights and to keep their money till they had some probability or assurance that it would be applied toward the support of the government, and that if they must fall a sacrifice to military force, they shall not be the first, but will bear it, for death itself was better than such slavery.[7]

The Ulster colonists had set the west on fire but, as in Boston, the authorities were not prepared to compromise. On 14 May 1771,

Governor Tyron of North Carolina led a force of militia to crush this Ulster uprising. At the Battle of Alamance River, nine settlers were killed and the rest of the protesters granted an amnesty. On 27 August, the *News Letter* reported on the aftermath of the rebellion in North Carolina:

> A number of the Regulators who were taken prisoner at the late battle with loyalists on the 16th May were tried and condemned, and that four of them had already been executed; one of whom had lost an arm in the engagement, and it is said was offered a pardon by the Governor if he would acknowledge his error, upon which condition he refused to accept it, saying that he would if at liberty, engage in the same cause again, and that had he had a loaded pistol he would blow out his Excellency's brains.[8]

Quiet was restored to the colonies, but the Sons of Liberty still existed and these same Ulster immigrants would be ready to rise again when the time was right. What was really significant was that lives had now been sacrificed for the cause that would be the lynchpin of America's revolution – liberty and justice – and that sacrifice had been made by the Ulster-American community. Sam Allen has concluded, "thus the first blood shed in the cause of American freedom was shed by Ulster-Scots at Alamance four years before Lexington".[9] William McKinley, America's twenty-fifth President and the great-great grandson of James McKinley from Conagher in County Antrim, said of these men who had laid down their lives:

> They were the first to proclaim for freedom in these United States: even before Lexington the Scotch-Irish blood had been shed for American freedom. In the forefront of every battle was seen their burnished mail and in the rear of retreat was heard their voice of constancy.[10]

It was not long before trouble flared up again with the capture and burning of *HMS Gaspee* by merchants from Newport, Rhode Island. The Royal Navy had been active in the area against smugglers and it was alleged that the commander had pressed men from the colony into service and had seized provisions from the inhabitants. Since local officials were not prepared to move against those responsible for the attack, the imperial government established a commission of investigation, comprising the governor of Rhode Island, the chief justice of New York, Massachusetts and New Jersey and a judge from the Vice-Admiralty court of New England. Although the commission was not as punitive as some had expected, it outraged the Sons of Liberty by proposing that all those arrested in connection with the incident should be tried in England. Again the cry of "English tyranny" was heard. The Virginia House of Burgesses now proposed the establishment of inter-colonial committees of correspondence to co-ordinate defence, along the lines of the network already established across Massachusetts by Sam Adams (by 1774, 300 towns in the colony had committees reporting to Boston, which was in contact with the radical movement in other regions).

The Gaspee incident was followed by the passing of the Tea Act in 1773, as the situation continued to deteriorate. The new Act removed the customs duty on the export of East Indian Company tea to America and also allowed the company to sell tea direct to the consumers. This was a blow to the smuggling trade and to the operation of colonial merchants and therefore to blow to colonial pride. However, the most galling thing about the Tea Act for Americans was that it was yet another arbitrary decision by the British government without consideration for or consultation with colonial opinion.

Massachusetts again took the lead with the local correspondence committee organising opposition to the Tea Act. Tensions were running especially high when three ships bearing cargoes of tea arrived in Boston harbour on 28 November. Samuel Adams and the radicals wanted the ships sent back, but Governor Hutchinson refused to authorise such an action. The wrangling went on for three weeks until the mob decided to take matters into their own hands. On 16 December, a party of radicals, some of whom were dressed as Indians, boarded the ships and dumped the tea chest into the water. The mob then made a triumphant march through the town. The "Boston Tea Party" has become part of American legend as well as American history and deservedly so. The *Belfast News Letter* kept its readers well informed about the events in Boston:

> there had been several meetings of the people of Boston, and that previous to the dissolution of the last, a number of persons

Top: *The burning of* HMS Gaspee, *June 1772.*
(Rhode Island Historical Society)
Bottom: *The Boston Tea Party. (Boston Picture Library)*

supposed to be the aboriginal natives from their complexion, approaching near the door of the assembly gave the war-whoop, which was answered by a few in the galleries of the house where the assembly was convened. Silence was commanded, and a prudent and peaceable deportment again enjoyed. The savages repaired to the ships which entertained the pestilential teas, and had begun their ravage previous to the dissolution of the meeting – they applied themselves to the destruction of this commodity in earnest, and in the space of about 2 hours broke up 342 chests, and discharged their contents into the sea. A watch was stationed to prevent embezzlement and not a single ounce of teas was suffered to be purloined by the populace.[11]

The example of Boston inspired Philadelphia to turn away teaships from Britain, while another "tea party" was held in New York the following year. In South Carolina, although tea was landed in Charles Town, the radicals prevented it being distributed. The *News Letter* reported:

Charles-Town, Nov 6. A few days since arrived the Britannica, Capt. Ball, from London. Notice having been received, that he had six chests of tea on board, near a thousand people were assembled on the wharf. They had prepared a scaffold two feet high to run on wheels, and placed thereon the Pope, Lord North, and the Pretender, in order to burn them with the tea; but as soon as the tea was brought upon deck the owners were ready with hatchets, and chopped the chests to pieces, and threw the tea overboard. The people then drew the scaffold about the town; and when it became dark, there was computed to be 2500 men with each a candle in his hand, who retired to the out parts of town, where they set fire to the scaffold; in the mean time some of them took the Pope's cap and went round to the ladies in the town, who emptied the tea out of their cannisters into the cap; they then burnt Lord North, the Pope, and Pretender, with the cap full of tea all together.[12]

The radical movement was now questioning not just parliament's right to tax, but its right to legislate at all. Governor Hutchinson of Massachusetts stated that there could be no compromise between the supreme authority of parliament and the total independence of the colonies. The response of the Massachusetts House of

Representatives was that by virtue of their charters the American colonies were states in their own right, although owing allegiance to the same monarch as Britain. As the situation deteriorated so the *News Letter* devoted more and more space to the growing crisis. Conscious of the strong link between Ulster and the American colonies, the paper kept its readers well informed about developments affecting their kith and kin across the Atlantic. The newspaper reproduced in full an address by the governor of Massachusetts to the General Assembly and on 16 March 1773, reproduced the reply presented by, among others, the inimitable John Hancock. The governor had stated the case of the Crown and now Hancock and his colleagues presented the case for the colonies, ending with this summation:

If your Excellency expects to have the line of distinction between the Supreme Authority of Parliament and the local Independence of the Colonies drawn by us, we would say that it would be a very arduous undertaking, and of very great importance to all other Colonies; and therefore could we conceive of such a line, we should be unwilling to propose it, without their consent in congress.

To conclude, these are great and profound questions. It is the grief of this house, that by the ill policy of a late injudicious administration, America has been driven into the contemplation of them. And we cannot but express our concern that your Excellency by your speech has reduced us to the unhappy alternative, either of appearing by our silence to acquiesce in your Excellency's sentiments, or of thus freely discussing this point. After all that we have said, we would be far from being understood to have in the least abated that just Sense of Allegiance which we owe to the King of Great Britain, our rightful Sovereign: and should the people of this province be left to the full and free exercise of all the liberties and immunities granted to them by charter, there would be no danger of an independence of the Crown. Our charter reserves great power to the Crown and its representatives fully sufficient to balance, analogous to the English Constitution, all the liberties and privileges granted to the people. All this your Excellency knows full well – And whoever considers the power and influence, in all their branches, reserved by our charter to the Crown, will be far from thinking that the Commons of this Province are too independent.[13]

This the British could not accept and it was now agreed in London that Massachusetts must be punished. In 1774, parliament passed a series of Coercive Acts which became known in America as the "Intolerable Acts". The Boston Port Act closed the port until compensation was paid by the town to the East Indian Company for the damage done to its property. An act was passed to regulate the government of the colony, establishing a provincial council which was to be appointed rather than elected. Furthermore, the governor was given sweeping powers under the terms of this act to appoint or remove judges, sheriffs and minor legal officials, to control the calling of town meetings and to supervise the jury system. An Act was passed to protect revenue and other crown officials in Massachusetts from intimidation and attack. The act even included the provision that should such officials be accused of capital crimes, in the performance of their duties, then they could be tried in Britain or another colony. The decision would be at the discretion of the governor. Finally, the Quartering Act allowed the governor to billet soldiers wherever he wanted. To ensure that the acts would be effectively enforced, Hutchinson was now replaced as governor of Massachusetts by the more resolute General Gage. Hutchinson's demise was closely monitored by the News Letter which reported in August 1773 that, "Governor Hutchinson has been burnt in effigy throughout America and it has become dangerous for him to venture out."[14] Later in the same month it was reported:

> The conduct of the Bostonians in their dispute with Governor Hutchinson has given great offence at St James's and it has been resolved upon to recall the Governor for the sake of his personal security.[15]

Although the Coercive Acts were criticised in parliament, by the likes of Charles Fox and Edmund Burke, the government was not to be deflected from its course.

In America, there also appeared to be no more room for compromise. Former moderates in the dispute between crown and colony, like Thomas Jefferson and George Washington, now joined the radicals in defending the colonies against what they saw as blatant British subversion. The radicals now began to drill and arm as well as to correspond and propagandise. In Massachusetts, General Gage was reluctant to even arrest any of the radical leaders because of the strength the movement now had in Boston. America was now preparing to fight for her beliefs and the whole country was mobilising. A letter dispatched to Ireland, dated 6 April 1774, by a recently arrived immigrant, caught the atmosphere of growing tension:

Since I arrived here I have taken some pains to learn the strength and disposition of our colonists; and had I not the most convincing proofs of the truth of what I here transmit to you, I should be silent on the subject. There is not a man here but what allots some part of the day for military exercise; and lads of thirteen, fourteen, and fifteen years of age, can use a gun with such dexterity, that it would surprize you; any of them can shoot a small bird flying with the greatest ease. Every man is also provided with a musket, sword, and bayonet; and as to their number, it is almost incredible. In every town and province they betray the same sentiments, that if the mother country treats them with severity, or sends soldiers over to annoy them, they will resist to the last drop of their blood.[16]

The settlers in many of the towns and counties of New England even drew up their own Solemn League and Covenant in their efforts to organise against Britain in the summer of 1774. These were the words and actions which would become familiar to later generations in the Ulster homeland.

In Virginia, the House of Burgesses was dissolved by the governor when it appealed for public support for Boston. The members then reconvened, unofficially, in Raleigh Tavern in Williamsburg and issued a call to all the other colonies to send delegates to a general congress to discuss the crisis. A nation was about to be born.

V

THE PEN AND THE SWORD

ON 5 September 1774, the first Continental Congress assembled in Philadelphia. All the colonies were represented, with the exception of Georgia. It was a historic occasion in every sense. The quality of the debates reflected the quality of the representatives, whose ability matched their determination.

There was general support for radical principles, especially in repudiating parliamentary supremacy. The consensus view was that the American colonies were equal members, with Britain, of an empire ruled by George III. Approval was given to a series of resolutions known as the Suffolk Resolves, which confirmed American opposition to the Coercive Acts and a Continental Association was established to enforce the agreed policy of non-importation from Britain. It was significant that the one plea for reconciliation with Britain, by the speaker of the Pennsylvania assembly, Joseph Galloway, was overwhelmingly rejected.

Following the stirrings of national resolve which had first appeared in the form of the Stamp Act Congress and the Committees of Correspondence, the American colonies had now taken a major step towards independence and colonial union.

In Britain, Lord North's ministry was in no mood to compromise following a general election which had consolidated its position. Indeed, the American situation had scarcely been mentioned in the political campaign and when Chatham presented a programme to deal with the growing crisis, including the repeal of all the acts unpopular in America and recognition of the Continental Congress as equivalent to parliament, his was truly a voice crying in the wilderness. The government had other policies in mind.

In 1775, the Restraining Act was passed banning all trade

*Paul Revere, on the famous ride that saved John Hancock
from capture by the British. (The Bettmann Archive)*

between the New England colonies and other British colonies and
also barring access to the fisheries of Newfoundland. This act was
shortly supplemented by another extending the provisions to all the
American colonies. These acts were quite simply undisguised
retaliation against the Continental Association's policy of non-
importation.

While pens on both sides of the Atlantic worked vigorously to
support the conflicting causes of Crown and Colony, preparations
were also underway to unsheathe the sword. The situation was
most tense in Massachusetts, where the radicals had been raising
money to buy arms and supplies in defiance of Governor Gage,
who was effectively besieged in Boston. This pattern was repeated
across the colonies.

Under pressure from the American Secretary, Lord Dartmouth,
Governor Gage decided to take the initiative and seize the radical's

supplies which were held in Concord, twenty miles from Boston. The British also hoped to capture John Hancock in Lexington, but he was warned in time by the ever vigilant Paul Revere. On 18 April 1775, 75 American volunteers, known as "Minute Men", barred the path of 700 British infantry at the village of Lexington. In the ensuing skirmish, eight Americans were killed and ten wounded. Although the British pressed on, the "Minute Men" had done their job, allowing time for the supplies in Concord to be removed by other patriots. American snipers continued to harass the British column as it made its way back to Boston. The Patriots also added insult to injury with their taunting cries of "King Hancock forever!" indicating the popular esteem in which the wealthy Boston merchant was held. Hancock was indeed a most wanted man, as evidenced by a report in the *Belfast News Letter* of 23–27 June 1775, which purported to be a verbatim account by a British officer of the events at Lexington and Concord:

> Tuesday evening, the 18th instant, the grenadiers and light infantry of the army received private orders to move from Boston at ten o'clock at night. They were passed over part of the harbour in boats; and on their landing proceeded on the road to Concord, a country town at the distance of twenty miles from hence. Our business was to seize a quantity of military stores, and – the bodies of Mess. Hancock and Adams, who are both attainted, and were at that place enforcing, by all their influence, the rebellious spirit of the Provincial Congress.[1]

Furthermore the *News Letter* reported the following on 21–25 July 1775:

> General Gage has issued a proclamation offering His Majesty's pardon to all persons who should immediately lay down their arms (except Samuel Adams and John Hancock) declaring all persons to be traitors who should aid and assist or hold any correspondence with rebels; and ordered martial law to be in force within the Province of Massachusetts Bay so long as the present unhappy occasion so necessarily requires it.[2]

Lexington and Concord made a deep impression on the Ulster mind, for people here were conscious that not only were their kith

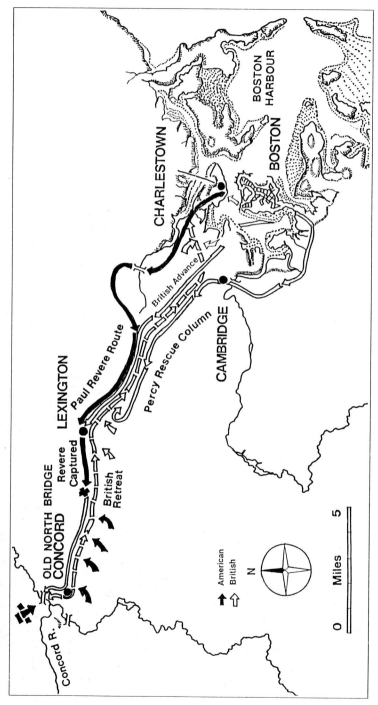

Map 2: *Lexington and Concord.*

Top: *The Battle of Lexington. (Connecticut Historical Society)*
Bottom: *The Battle of Lexington. (US Navy)*

The Fight on the Bridge at Concord. (Culver Pictures)

and kin now at war, but they were fighting for principles and beliefs which they all shared. No better example of this bond can be found than in a toast delivered at a dinner in Tandragee, in July 1775, celebrating the battle of Aughrim. Glasses were raised to:

> The memory of the saints and martyrs, that fell at Lexington on the 19th April last in America. May the tyranny and persecution their fathers fled from in Europe never fasten on their sons in America.[3]

At times the conflict in America had overtones and indeed close ties to the sectarian conflict in Ulster. In stark contrast to the fact that many of the American "rebels" were Ulster Protestants, the *Belfast News Letter* of 11 to 15 May 1775 reported that an Irish nobleman had made an offer to the British authorities "to raise 5,000 Roman Catholics, to support their plan against the Americans".[4] Another example of this reversal of the traditional roles played by the Ulster Protestants and Roman Catholics was demonstrated in a letter printed in the *Belfast News Letter* of 8 April 1778:

To the KING's most excellent Majesty. The humble address of the Roman Catholics of the town of Newry in your Majesty's kingdom of Ireland.

We, the Roman Catholics of the town of Newry, with hearts full of gratitude, humbly presume to lay at the foot of the throne our most sincere acknowledgements for the indulgence and protection we enjoy under your Majesty's humane goverment.

We humbly beg leave to assure your Majesty, that the undutiful, obstinate, and ungenerous perservance of America gives us heartfelt grief. We feel for the distresses of the parent state like afflicted sons; and weep that tears are the only arms allowed to support the rights and dignity of the crown and constitution of Great Britain.

At the present alarming and unexpected crisis, when enemies seem to multiply, and hostilities threaten this country and every thing dear to us, we think it an indispensible duty humbly to approach the throne, with the most unfeigned assurances of our violable allegiance to your Majesty's royal person and government; and with all sincerity of heart to declare, that we are willing, by every means in our power, to contribute to the defence of the honour and dignity of your crown, and the constitution of England, against all enemies who would attempt to disturb the state or invade this kingdom.

Given under our hands, at a public meeting, the 8th April, 1778.[5]

In stark contrast James McHenry wrote to his friend in Belfast on 23 March 1778.

State of Virginia, Williamsburgh, March 23d, 1778

My Dear Sir,

The long interruption our correspondence has suffered by the separation of the colonies from Britain, has neither altered my friendship for you, nor the affection I bear to the country which gave me birth. This is a natural affection, and superceded only by my strong attachment to freedom, and hatred of tyranny. It is this which early engaged me and so many of our countrymen in the American cause.

The little time I have to spare will not permit me to enter into a detail of our last year's operations;– the success of our arms under

General Gates and the vigorous efforts we made against Gen. Howe, until he was finally besieged in Philadelphia. He is now shut up (as he was in Boston) by an army greatly superior to his in point of numbers and strength. Add to this, that fresh levys from our different states are in the greatest forwardness, while the most effectual measures are pursuing for an early and conclusive campaign. You may be assured that I am not holding up delusive or exaggerated accounts: I speak from observation, and in the confidence of friendship. This year will, in all probability, put an end to the war, by the final establishment of our independence. Depend upon it, all the power that your King can muster from the four corners of his dominions, will not be able to procure him other terms. Independence is become to Americans what Magna Charta is to a true-born Englishman. Let England therefore make peace while she may, if she has yet left the poor ambition of continuing a monarchy; for we are now convinced that we have nothing to fear from the force of Britain or the intrigues of France.

God bless you. _____ Remember me to my relations, and believe me to be your's most affectionately. JAMES McHENRY.[6]

The *News Letter* also took some pleasure in reproducing in its issue of the 8-12 September 1775 a poem from the *Dublin Mercury* by a certain James Hoey, whom it described as a "Popish News-Printer":

On the accounts published in the Belfast Journal, relative to the present State of America.

The puritan-journal, impress'd at Belfast,
    Exhibits the printer's complexion and cast;
Whole partial accounts of each public transaction
    Proclaim him the infamous tool of a faction.

From worthy old Faulkner, to give him his due,
    Nought issues, but what is authentic and true;
Each foreign report and domestic relation
    Approv'd and admitted on good information.

But ***, the low scribe of a party quite frantic
    With zeal for their brethren beyond the Atlantic,

General Henry Knox. (Museum of Fine Arts, Boston)

Discreetly and piously chuses to tell
    No tidings, but such as come posting from hell:

Thence furnished with news, it is easy to guess
    Why nothing but falsehoods proceed from his press;
Of which he is sure to have constant supplies,
    Who still correspond with the father of lies.[7]

Lexington and Concord could not really be claimed as a victory
by either side, but they were significant in confirming that a state of

war now existed. Soon fighting flared up in Virginia, where the British seized patriot supplies at Williamsburg, while the Americans captured the strategic fortress of Ticonderoga. Ticonderoga fell on 10 May 1775, resulting in the capture of much British artillery which would soon be put to good use in the siege of Boston by a certain Henry Knox. The son of a County Antrim family, Knox was a book seller by profession in Boston. He was destined, however, to leave the world of books far behind him. Richard Morris acknowledges the achievement of Knox in re-deploying the British artillery in the developing siege of Boston:

> by prestigious efforts Henry Knox managed to load nearly 60 cannon, including mortars that weighed a ton, on ox drawn sledges and bring them over the rivers and mountains to the siege of Boston in early '76.[8]

On 10 May, the second Continental Congress gathered in Philadelphia to plan and prepare for the fight that lay ahead. One of the most important decisions to be taken was the appointment of a commander of the patriot forces. John Hancock had hoped to be offered the post but the decision to appoint George Washington proved to be a crucial factor in America's eventual victory.

At the same time as the congress was preparing for war, the Ulster-Americans were again thinking ahead and preparing for independence. The General Synod of the Presbyterian Church was also meeting in Philadelphia and it issued a pastoral letter, to all Presbyterian congregations, whose tone strengthened colonial resolve and gave a lead to Congress. The *News Letter* quoted the following extract:

> It is well known to you (otherwise it would be imprudent thus publically to profess) that we have not been instrumental in inflaming the minds of the people, or urging them to acts of violence and disorder. Perhaps no instance can be given on so interesting a subject, in which political sentiments have been so long and so fully kept from the pulpit, and even malice itself has not charged us with labouring from the press; but things are now come to such a height, that we do not wish to conceal our opinions as men. Suffer us therefore to exhort you, by assuring you that there is no army so formidable, as those who are superior to the feat of

death. Let therefore every one who, from generousity of spirit, or benevolence of heart, offers himself as a champion in his country's cause, be persuaded to reverence the Lord of Hosts, and walk in the fear of the Prince of Kings of the Earth, and then he may, with the most unshaken firmness, expect the issue either in death or victory.[9]

On 31 May 1775, a gathering of Ulster immigrants in Charlotte, Mecklenburg County, North Carolina, drew up a series of resolutions which unequivocally stated America's case. The "Mecklenburg Resolutions" were, in effect, a declaration of independence almost a year before congress drafted and approved the great declaration. These resolutions were drafted and proposed by Doctor Ephriam Brevard, an Ulster-Huguenot, and the meeting was chaired by Thomas Polk whose family came from the Londonderry-Donegal border. W. F. Marshall also makes mention of the Ulster-Americans taking a similar initiative further north:

> A similar Declaration of Independence was issued by the people of Ulster origin and descent in New Hampshire and this declaration also preceded the Declaration of Congress.[10]

The ink had scarcely dried on these pages before the scene again switched to the field of battle at Bunker Hill, overlooking Boston harbour. This was an important strategic point which General Gage decided to attack on 17 June 1775. The American volunteers were under the command of Israel Putnam and their fierce resistance cost the British dearly. Although Gage captured the hill, he lost 226 men dead and 826 wounded, compared to American losses of 140 dead, 270 wounded and 30 captured. Numbered among the ranks of the American defenders were two men of Ulster-American stock from New Londonderry in New Hampshire. Colonel John Stark, whose father had arrived in the colonies in 1719, was destined to rise to the rank of Commander in Chief of the Northern Department of the US Army by 1781 and his colleague, General George Reid, would also gain fame as one of Washington's fighting Ulster-American generals. Bunker Hill also focused the spot-light more directly on Henry Knox, heralding his rapid rise to fame and glory. Henry Jones Ford has written of the man who would later become America's first Secretary of War:

> At the Battle of Bunker Hill Knox acted as a staff officer,

The Battle of Bunker Hill. (US Navy)

reconnoitering the British movements. During the campaign that followed he was active in planning and constructing works of defence for the various positions held by the Americans. His ability as a military engineer and as an artillerist attracted attention and obtained General Washington's esteem. On November 17, 1775, although Knox was only twenty-five years old, he was commissioned Colonel of the only artillery regiment in the Continental Army. He served throughout the war with distinction, enjoying the steady confidence and friendship of Washington. He took part in all important engagements down to the siege of Yorktown, his arrangements for which were such that Washington reported to the President of Congress that "the resources of his genius supplied the deficit of means".[11]

Henry Steele Commager points out that Knox, "grew in stature over the years" and with Nathaniel Green was the only officer that Washington "trusted implicitly".[12] Proof of this fact would later be seen in Washington's emotional farewell to his officers at Fraunces Tavern on 4 December 1783, when Knox was singled out as the first officer to receive the Commander in Chief's embrace.

British success at Bunker Hill was illusory. Apart from the fact that they had suffered much heavier casualties than the Americans, it soon became clear that Gage could not hold his position for any length of time. By 1776, the British were faced by a strong and tenacious American force, strengthened with artillery captured at Ticonderoga. Gage's only option seemed to be withdraw and that is what he did on 17 March, moving his army, accompanied by loyalist civilians, to Halifax, Nova Scotia. The British army had left the soil of Massachusetts, never to return.

The war, however, was to continue. General Gage was replaced as British Commander in Chief by William Howe and the army was reinforced by 18,000 European mercenaries. These included recruits from Hesse-Cassel in Germany, who would soon acquire an infamous reputation for their ruthlessness. Further British initiatives included a blockade of all American ports by the Royal Navy and a plan to attack New York. The last hope for a peaceful settlement quickly disappeared with parliament's rejection of what became known as the "Olive Branch Petition" from congress.

America's response was to prepare for independence. Support for such action had been growing steadily with each clash with Britain

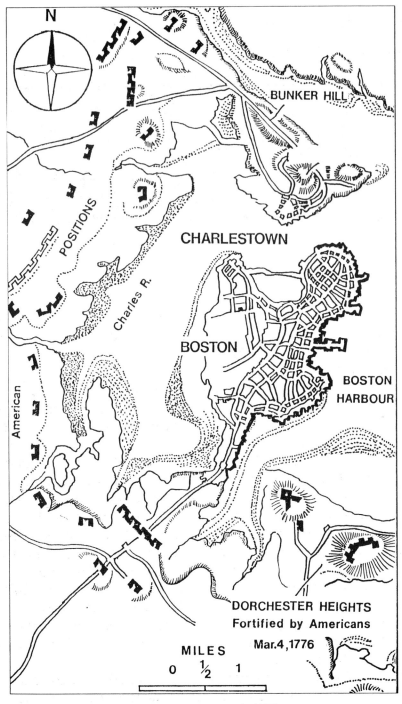

Map 3: *Boston, March 1776.*

The British evacuate Boston in March 1776, under threat from the guns of Henry Knox. (New York Historical Society)

and of course there was already the example set by the Ulster-American community in North Carolina, who had shed their blood at the Alamance River in 1771 and attached their names to the famous Mecklenburg Resolutions in 1775.

The argument for independence was further enhanced by the publication, in January 1776, of a pamphlet entitled *Common Sense*. This was the work of a recent English immigrant called the Tom Paine. Its revolutionary message struck a chord with American people, reflected in the sale of 120,000 copies. Paine argued that the price of revolution was only worth paying if it was carried to the extent of creating an independent republic – the repeal of unpopular acts and the replacement of the present British government would not solve the basic problem of America being ruled unjustly by a remote monarch and his chosen ministers. Paine's emphasis on giving recognition only to the monarchy of God was particularly popular with the Ulster Presbyterians. George Washington felt the pamphlet made a convincing case for the abolition of the crown and independence from Britain. It was clear that the time had now come to settle the question of how America was going to be governed.

The Continental Congress now proceeded to authorise the establishment of a new system of government for the provinces. The new governments, so established, in turn began to press for

Two of the men who voted for independence greet outside Independence Hall – on the right, Caesar Rodney and on the left, the Ulster-American, Thomas McKean. (Herbert Orth)

independence through their delegates in congress. There was clear recognition that America was one nation and that the congress and the provinces must work together.

The mind of congress began to concentrate on drafting a declaration of independence and a committee was selected to carry out this task. The individuals in question were Benjamin Franklin of Pennsylvania, John Adams of Massachusetts, Rodger Sherman of Connecticut, Robert Livingston of New York and Thomas Jefferson of Virginia. The idea of the declaration had been advocated by Tom Paine and in many respects was a natural follow-up to John Dickinson's *Declaration of the Causes and Necessity of Taking Up Arms,* which had been produced a year earlier.

The task of composing the declaration fell to Jefferson, whose brilliant mind and gift for writing made him eminently suited to the job. His legal training and experience also meant that he was well qualified to present America's case effectively. He had a draft ready

The Declaration of Independence. (Library of Congress)

for presentation at the end of June 1776.

On 2 July, the main resolutions were accepted by congress when they were presented by Richard Henry Lee of Virginia. To all intents and purposes, this day really marks America's break with Britain, but the final ratification of the entire document was given by congress two days later, on 4 July 1776.

Congress approached the act of declaring independence in a solemn and religious manner, reflecting their Protestant faith. The *News Letter* of 6–10 September 1776 reported on the events in Philadelphia:

> The 4th of July, 1776, the Americans appointed as a day of fasting and prayer, preparatory to their dedicating their country to God, which was done in the following manner: The Congress being assembled after having declared America independent, they had a crown placed on a bible, which by prayer and solemn devotion they offered to God. This religious ceremony being ended, they divided the crown into thirteen parts, each of the United Provinces taking a part.[13]

The final draft was a masterpiece which stood the test of time, although congress did make some alterations to Jefferson's text. The greater part of the document was made up of a list of complaints against George III, preserving the Whig myth that bad government was the fault of the Crown.

The concluding charge was that it had been the plan of the King to establish an absolute monarchy in America. The preamble to this list of charges was truly memorable, as an eloquent and poetic assertion of the rights of man. Indeed, it remains an inspiration to the American nation to this day and ensured that the Declaration would find a permanent place in history.

The introductory section of the Declaration also reflected the experience of the American people. They had created government institutions from scratch and, with the immigrants from Ulster playing a leading role, had created civilization out of the wilderness. The democratic spirit of the document owed much to the Ulster heritage of many of the new citizens of America.

The Declaration of Independence and the American revolution can be seen as the natural culmination of the forces which had initially led to the emergence of the colonies and which were at the

The men who signed the Declaration of Independence, seven of whom were of Ulster descent. (US Capital Historical Society) – see key below.

Key: 1. William Whipple. 2. Robert Treat Paine. 3. Thomas Nelson. 4. Charles Thompson. 5. John Hancock. 6. Edward Rutledge. 7. Thomas McKean.

very heart of the Ulster community – the Protestant Reformation, the thirst for education and scientific development and the quest for political progress. Jefferson's statement of human equality became an inspiration to the movements for reform and revolution in Europe and gave Americans a sense of national identity. It was entirely fitting that 4 July became and remained a landmark in American history, celebrated in the years to come with great patriotic fervour, involving speeches, parades and social events.

It was also appropriate that Ulster-Americans played a key role in the production of the document, for their community was its bedrock. The draft sanctioned by congress was transcribed by Charles Thompson of Maghera in County Londonderry, who held the rank of Perpetual Secretary to the Continental Congress. There were 56 signatories to the Declaration and eight of these men were of Ulster ancestry. The most famous was undoubtedly John Hancock of Massachusetts, who had been in the vanguard of the movement for liberty from its inception and who now held the rank of President of Congress. Hancock's signature was the first on the document and it was also the largest, for it was reputed that King George could not see very well and he wanted to make sure that his name was not missed. On completing his signature, Hancock is reputed to have quipped, "There, I guess King George will be able to read that." The seven other Ulster-Americans who championed America's cause were William Whipple, whose parents had arrived in Maine in 1730; Robert Paine, whose grandfather came from Dungannon; Thomas McKean, whose father came from Ballymoney; Thomas Nelson, whose grandfather came from Strabane; Matthew Thornton, who had settled in New Londonderry in New Hampshire in 1718; George Taylor, the son of an Ulster-Presbyterian minister and Edward Rutledge, another son of an Ulster immigrant family.

After being transcribed, debated and signed in congress, the Declaration was then passed into the hands of another Ulsterman to be printed. John Dunlap had come from a well-known printing business in Strabane to start work in America earlier in the century. He had actually been born in Strabane in 1764 and he now had the signal honour of printing the first copies of the great document. Dunlap was indeed to enhance his fame and his place in history when he printed America's first daily newspaper in 1784, the *Pennsylvania Packet*.

As well as being printed, the Declaration of Independence was also read in public across America. George Washington ordered that it should be read to all American troops. The very first public reading was made by Colonel John Nixon, whose father had sailed from Ulster to America some year earlier. The complete text of the Declaration was printed in the *Belfast News Letter* of 23–27 August 1776, making it the first paper outside America to do so.

The American Declaration of Independence then has many links with Ulster and it is surely one of Ulster's proudest legacies, as Hugh Brogan has remarked, ". . . the Declaration was a protest and a programme, not only for Jefferson's countrymen, but for civilized mankind".[14]

Articles of Confederation were now drawn up by the Continental Congress, granting formal recognition to government arrangements already in operation. Power was now conferred on congress to appoint ministers and carry out agreed policies. Eight of the thirteen united states drew up new constitutions for themselves, in which the balance of power was held by the legislature and in which hereditary public offices were largely abolished. Other reforms which were carried included a Bill of Rights, a redistribution of land (at the expense of loyalists) and the annulment of the British Proclamation of 1763, limiting the western expansion of the colonies. The emphasis on democracy reflected the mood of the time and the spirit of the Ulster-American people.

VI

FREE AT LAST

AMERICA had now proclaimed her independence but the war had still to be won. As the winter of 1776 came on, the Patriots were encouraged by Washington's victories in the battles of Trenton and Princeton in December. These clashes may have been small in terms of numbers involved but their significance really lay in their value to the Americans in terms of strategy and morale. New Jersey and Pennsylvania were now secured for the Patriots, following a period in which the British had been making steady progress under General Howe through Long Island, Manhattan and New Jersey.

American joy at these successes in the middle states, however, was tempered somewhat by defeat in the north. Here, a two-pronged campaign against Quebec reached its climax on the last day of December 1775. The American attack was commanded by General Benedict Arnold, approaching from Maine and Brigadier-General Richard Montgomery, approaching from Montreal. Montgomery was born near Convoy in County Donegal and was a British-trained officer who had served with the 17th Regiment of Foot. Described by Commager as "the ablest of the early senior officers",[1] Montgomery had scored notable success in this campaign with the capture of St. Johns, in which he had captured the colours of the 7th Fusiliers, the first British flags to fall to the Americans in the war. Montreal had also capitulated to Montgomery on 13 November 1775. It was therefore a confident army that reached Quebec late in December and one in which Richard Montgomery was but the leader of a significant Ulster-American contingent. Montgomery's colleague, General Michael Simpson, was another Ulsterman, while the ranks of Benedict Arnold's force included one company of Ulster-American riflemen from Virginia under the

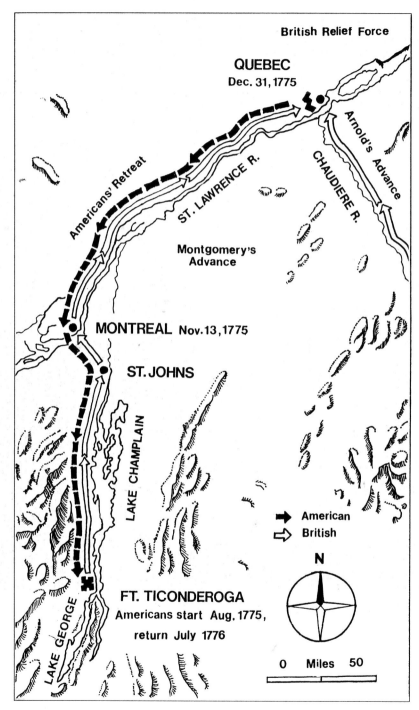

Map 4: *Quebec, December 1775.*

The death of Richard Montgomery at Quebec. (Yale University Art Gallery)

command of Dan Morgan, another Ulsterman of whom much more would be heard later. Morgan, in fact, was captured in the attack on Quebec, in which the Americans lost 100 men dead or wounded and over 300 taken prisoner. Benedict Arnold was wounded in the battle but the greatest blow to the American cause was Montgomery's death, the victim of a lucky shot by a drunken British sailor. Although the British, under Sir Guy Carleton, had saved Quebec, the American challenge had not entirely been in vain for the Redcoats now had to postpone their plans to take the offensive.

Montgomery's death was honoured by Congress on 26 January 1776 with the decision to erect a Cenotaph in his memory. The *News Letter* of 18–22 March reproduced the inscription that the memorial would bear:

> Montgomery falls! Let no fond breast repine
>   That Hampden's glorious death, brave chief, was thine.
> With his, shall freedom consecrate thy name,
>   Shall date her rising glories from thy fame,
> Shall build her throne of empire on thy grave;
>   – What nobler fate can patriot virtue crave![2]

The scene of action now switched to New York, where there was a stand-off between the opposing sides. The Americans were in a difficult position, as General Joseph Reed, the son of an Ulster family who had settled in New Jersey and Washington's adjutant-general, acknowledged:

> We cannot stay and yet we do not know how to go – so that we may be properly said to be between hawk and buzzard.[3]

Eventually the Patriot forces were obliged to withdraw. It was a low point in the war for the Americans and one which encouraged much back-biting. Henry Knox despaired that the Patriot army was little better than, "a receptacle of ragamuffins".[4] As the war now entered another new year, George III and his ministers became increasingly impatient for final victory. Under pressure from London, General Burgoyne now decided to take the initiative and to split the Patriot army while leading a force of 7,000 men from Canada to the Hudson River. It was undoubtedly a bold plan but to succeed it required close co-ordination and co-operation from

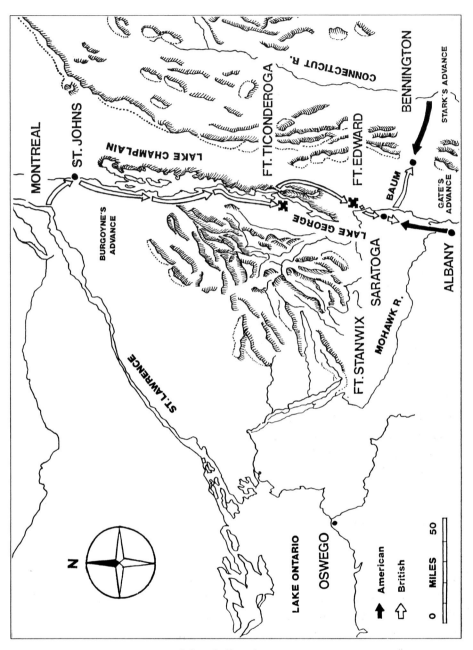

Map 5: *Bennington.*

General Howe. This proved to be a stumbling block for the whole operation, with disastrous consequences for the loyalist cause.

Howe had his sights set on Philadelphia and was not prepared to wait on Burgoyne's ponderous approach. The latter's progress was further hampered by attacks from the American militia. The most significant of these clashes occurred at the Battle of Bennington on 16 August 1777, when Colonel John Stark led 2,000 of his "Green Mountain Boys" against Lieutenant Colonel Friedrich Baum's wing. Stark, a doughty veteran of the French and Indian wars, had vowed before the battle, "We will beat them before night or Molly Stark will be a widow."[5] He kept his word in a battle which saw the Loyalist Commander Baum killed and British reinforcements thrown back. In recognition of his great victory, Stark, who had earlier resigned his commission because congress had promoted a number of junior officers over his head, now was given the rank of brigadier. This son of Ulster would go on to serve the American cause well.

The battle at Bennington was referred to in the *News Letter* of 28–31 October 1777, taking its detail from a letter recently received from America:

> On Col. Baume's arrival near Bennington, finding the number of the rebels far to exceed what was expected; he posted himself very advantageously, and sent to Gen. Burgoyne for a reinforcement, but in the mean time the rebels to the amount of 4000, attacked him and precipitately surrounded him so closely, that they (the rebels) dare not discharge their pieces for fear of doing mischief to their own people; before they recovered from this mistake, our troops made great slaughter among them, but being overpowered by numbers, they were at length obliged to retire with the loss of 200 killed, wounded and taken prisoners after a most gallant defence, shewing an intrepidity and determined resolution, not to be expected in such a mixed body of Savages, Canadians, &c. supported by so few regular soldiers.[6]

Bennington, in fact, turned out to be the overture to a much greater American victory. Burgoyne's army had been greatly weakened and, with their supplies almost exhausted, it was no match for the Patriot army facing them under General Horatio Gates. The Battle of Saratoga, on 17 October 1777, was a devastating

Colonel John Stark. (Culver Pictures)

*Hessian prisoners are led off the field by John Stark's men after
the Battle of Bennington, 16 August 1777. (Culver Pictures)
Bottom: The surrender of Burgoyne to General Gates
at Saratoga. (Fort Ticonderoga Museum)*

American victory in which a significant role was again played by
Dan Morgan's Virginia riflemen. Indeed, after Burgoyne had
surrendered to Gates he acknowledged to Morgan, "Your Scotch-
Irish rifles is the finest in the world."[7] Historian Henry Steele
Commager has concluded:

> Daniel Morgan's riflemen with their deadly marksmanship were
> the most successful units to appear.[8]

The *News Letter* of 16–19 December 1777 carried a full report on
Saratoga and listed the Articles of Convention agreed on the
surrender of General Burgoyne. The paper had first reported news
of the British defeat in the issue 18–21 November.

After Saratoga, the fall of Philadelphia to General Howe seemed
an easy burden for the Americans to bear. However, during Howe's
advance on the town, the Americans had suffered severe casualties
in a night attack at Paoli. The Patriots lost about 300 men to British

Top: *The surrender of Burgoyne to General Gates
at Saratoga. (Fort Ticonderoga Museum)*

Bottom: *The Paoli massacre – Anthony Wayne's troops are taken
by surprise by the British. (Valley Forge Historical Society)*

bayonets and a question mark was raised over the preparedness of the American commander. The Paoli Massacre was covered in the *News Letter* of 5–9 December 1777, quoting a British Army report:

> Upon intelligence that General Wayne was lying in the woods with a corps of fifteen hundred men, and four pieces of cannon, about three miles distant, and in the rear of the left wing of the army, Major-General Grey was detached on the 20th late at night, with the 2d light infantry, the 42d and 44th regiments, to surprize, this corps, the most effectual precaution being taken by the General to prevent his detachment from firing, he gained the enemy's left about one o'clock; and having, by the bayonet only, forced their out-sentries and pickets, he rushed in upon their encampment, directed by the light of their fires, killed and wounded not less than three hundred on the spot, taking between seventy and eighty prisoners, including several officers the greater part of their arms, and eight wagons loaded with baggage and stores. Upon the first alarm, the cannon were carried off, and the darkness of the night only saved the remainder of the corps:– One Captain of the light infantry and three men were killed in the attack and four men wounded. Gallantry in the troops and good conduct in the General, were fully manifested upon this critical service.[9]

General Anthony Wayne, whose grandfather had fought under William III at the Boyne, was one of Washington's most daring cavalry commanders. The massacre at Paoli, on the night of 20-21 September 1777, however, led some to accuse him of being negligent in his duty. Wayne refused to bow to such attacks and his stance was vindicated at a subsequent court martial, when he was cleared of all charges "with the highest Honour".[10] Wayne would continue to serve Washington and serve him well.

The way was now clear for the British to advance into Philadelphia but it was to be a short lived success. The town was abandoned by the King's men in the following year, following the pattern of short term British successes.

The main impact the British advances had on the Americans was in forcing Washington's army to spend the winter of 1777–78 in terrible conditions at the Valley Forge camp, where both food and clothing were scarce. The French officer, Lafayette, commented on the Patriots' plight:

General Anthony Wayne – "Mad Anthony" was the grandson of one of William III's veterans at the Boyne. (New York Historical Society)

The American encampment in Valley Forge, Virginia, during the winter of 1777–78. (New York State Historical Association)

They have neither coats, hats, shirts or shoes; their feet and legs froze until they became black.[11]

As American morale sank lower with the deepening of winter, many soldiers deserted the cause. Only the hardiest remained and it was possibly at this point that Washington paid his famous tribute to the Ulster-American fighters:

If defeated everywhere else, I will make my last stand for liberty among the Scotch-Irish of my native Virginia.[12]

Washington's statement reflects the fact that within America at this time it has been estimated that about one-third of the population were loyal to the crown, one-third were waverers and one-third patriots. The Ulster-American contribution in the fight for freedom was therefore vital. W. F. Marshall reinforces the point:

There were times, therefore, when this army was small, but since it is generally agreed that the Ulster-Irish were steadfastly enthusiastic for the war, it could very well be that often they compromised the greater part of his men. One famous force of regulars was the Pennsylvania Line and these were Ulster-Irish almost to a man.[13]

Henry Jones Ford provides further evidence of Washington's debt to the Ulster-Americans:

The origin of all the officers of the revolutionary army cannot be determined with sufficient accuracy to admit of any statistical exhibit, but Scotch-Irish of Ulster nativity were so numerous that a provision of the Constitution of the United States was drawn to meet their case. When the qualifications for membership in the House of Representatives were considered in the convention it was in question whether natives only should be eligible or else how long a term of citizenship should be prerequisite. In the course of the debate Wilson of Pennsylvania remarked that "almost all the general officers of the Pennsylvania line of the late army were foreigners," and he mentioned that three members of the Pennsylvania delegation in the convention, he himself being one, were not natives. The term was finally fixed at seven years in the Revolutionary War, whether native born or not. The immigrants thus provided for were mainly Scotch-Irish.[14]

A letter from an officer in one of the Highland regiments remarked upon the significance of the Ulster element in the make-up of the forces ranged against the crown:

The country is chiefly in the hands of emigrants from New York, and two or three townships from the North of Ireland. The Americans and Irish Dissenters in this province are to a man disaffected to government. The few English and Scots, the Germans, and Irish Roman Catholics, would wish to live in peace, and I believe would take arms on the side of the mother country.[15]

While the Ulster-American soldiers endured the trials of Valley Forge, help was on its way from the Old World. Throughout 1777–78, America had been negotiating for an alliance with France. The Patriots had already been receiving support from the French in the form of secret arms shipments, but Benjamin Franklin now sought to bring France herself into the war. The United States could not have had a better advocate than the worthy Dr Franklin, a man whose reputation for scientific work preceded him and endeared him to the *Academie des Sciences*, where he was embraced by Voltaire. His manner and dress also made him a popular figure in Paris society. The French government needed little persuading to support America's cause, with the foreign minister, Bergennes, particularly enthusiastic. The only voice of caution was that of Turgot, the former controller-general of finances, who felt France, in the wake of the Seven Years War, could not afford another conflict with Britain. Any doubts the French may have had were finally dispelled at Saratoga and France officially became America's ally in 1778, later to be joined by both Spain and Holland.

Support for the French alliance was by no means universal, as the *News Letter* observed in an extract reprinted from the *New York Gazette* of 17 February 1779:

> The people daily grow more and more disaffected to the Congress's alliance with a Popish King, and their disgust has greatly increased since the publication of a resolution of that body, published in our last Gazette, which implies the most abject dependence upon the will and pleasure of their great and good ally, Louis the XVIth.[16]

While America may have been uncertain about who it should choose as friends, the *News Letter* reported in its issue of 12–15 May 1778 on the decision of the new nation upon a new flag:

> The American Congress has resolved, "That the flag of the Thirteen United States be thirteen stripes, alternative red and white; that the union be thirteen stars, white on a blue field, representing a new constellation."[17]

The nature of the war was altered quite dramatically by the entry of France and Spain. British supply lines across the Atlantic were now even more vulnerable to attack and the very existence of Britain's empire soon transformed the conflict into a world war. Unlike the Seven Years War, when Britain could count on France being diverted by her continental clash with Frederick II of Prussia, she now stood isolated facing not only the combined power of

France, Spain and Holland, but also the threat of an even more extensive conflict under the auspices of the newly created League of Armed Neutrality, led by Catherine II of Russia.

France was now able to take the initiative with attacks on British possessions in the Caribbean, North America and India. Indeed, Britain's fear of losing the profitable Sugar Islands, which she had captured during the Seven Years War, led to the Caribbean becoming the main theatre of war. At the same time Spain captured Minorca and besieged Gibraltar.

Britain's plight in this "new" war was highlighted by the capture of HMS *Serapis* by the American raider *Bonhomme Richard*, under the captaincy of John Paul Jones. British shipping losses at the hands of the Americans were to total £18 million. Of course, it was not all one-way traffic. The British war effort was boosted by America's rejection of peace proposals which would have conceded all demands except that for independence. The Royal Navy sought out and attacked American shipping and also launched assaults against coastal areas like Newhaven and Richmond, Virginia. In fact, the new Governor of Virginia, Thomas Jefferson, was driven out of the new state capital by a force led by the traitor, Benedict Arnold in January 1781. The previous year had also seen General Clinton attack Charlestown (now Charleston) in South Carolina.

If Britain was not going to give up without a fight then the Americans and especially the Ulster-Americans, were ready and able to provide that fight. In 1777, an American campaign was launched under the command of General George Rogers Clark, who came from an Ulster family in the Valley of Virginia. Clark was a 25-year-old surveyor and amateur archaeologist and also a noted Indian fighter. He had four brothers who served as officers in the Continental Army. One of these was William, who would later earn fame as joint commander of the Lewis-Clark expedition which explored the far west in the years 1804 to 1806.

George Rogers Clark won the backing of the Virginia government for a mission to save the frontier settlements in Kentucky from British-backed Indian attacks. Leading his small force of 175 men across 180 miles of swamp and forest, Clark reached his goal in July 1778. Despite the hardships they had suffered, Clark's force captured Kaskaskia, Cahokia and Vincennes. The latter fort was later recovered by a joint force of British, Canadians and Indians under Lieutenant Governor Hamilton, but Clark was not to be

General George Rogers Clark (Brown Brothers)

Top: *George Rogers Clark's expedition across 180 miles of treacherous terrain would climax in victory at Kaskaskia, Cahokia and Vincennes on the frontier. (Culver Pictures)*

Bottom: *General James Clinton's men head up the Susquehanna river valley to join John Sullivan's expedition against the Iroquois. (Canajoharie Library)*

disappointed and, displaying all the tenacity typical of the Ulster Americans, he forced the garrison to surrender and took Hamilton prisoner.

The war against Britain's Indian allies brought another Ulsterman to the fore in 1779, when General James Clinton, a native of Ulster and the defender of Fort Clinton, played a key role in General Sullivan's campaign. The target on this occasion was the Iroquois tribe, who had been responsible for massacres in Wyoming and Cherry valleys. Sullivan and Clinton swept up the Susquehanna River to clear the territory of their enemies.

In the same year, General Anthony Wayne reappeared to lead an attack against Stoney Point, which was the key to the lower Hudson valley. On 17 July 1779, Wayne lived up to his nickname of "Mad Anthony" when he ordered his 1,350 troops to charge uphill with their guns unloaded, to ensure stealth and surprise. The tactic was a startling success with the British quickly surrendering at the points of the Ulster-American bayonets. General Wayne detailed his victory in a letter of 17 July 1779 to John Jay, which the News Letter published in its issue of 5–8 October 1779. The same paper also reported the thanks of Congress for Wayne's victory, expressed in the following resolution:

> Resolved: That the thanks of Congress be presented to Brigadier-General Wayne, for his brave, prudent and soldierly conduct, in the spirited and well conducted attack on Stoney Point.[18]

Beaten in the north, General Cornwallis now turned his eyes to the south where he was sure there was a better prospect of victory. In 1780, the British invaded Georgia, North Carolina and South Carolina. They were determined to bring Washington's army to what they confidently expected would be a successful show down. They were equally confident that France was not as well-equipped as Britain to withstand the strain of a long war.

While Cornwallis may have been right about the French, it soon became clear that the longer the war continued the larger and stronger Washington's army became. Those who had been neutral at the outset were now inspired to join the Patriot cause by the spirit of the Declaration of Independence, the military successes against the British, the atrocities committed by Britain's Iroquois allies in the north-west and by Britain's callous abandonment of American

*The Americans overrun the British at Stoney Point in the Hudson
Valley – a brilliant victory for "Mad Anthony" Wayne.
(New York State Historical Association)*

loyalists to their fate. Some of these left for Britain, but about 80,000 refugees moved north to Lake Erie, to become the bed-rock of English-speaking Canada.

Perhaps the chief factor in swinging the balance of the war, at this stage, in favour of the Americans was the reaction against the brutal campaign conducted by the British in the south, under the likes of Banastre Tarleton. A young man by the name of Andrew Jackson was one of many Ulster-Americans who would harbour bitter memories of this period.

The Americans responded with successful guerrilla attacks, organised by the likes of Dan Morgan and his fellow Ulster-American, Andrew Pickens. Commager makes mention of two other Ulster-American forces which made life difficult for the British:

> William R Davie, at the head of the "Bloody Corps" in Mecklenburg County, and William Lee Davidson, with his Scotch-Irish legion from Catawba, made Cornwallis's march into North Carolina equally expensive ... The war in the South, like the war in the West, became a grim struggle marked by viciousness and brutality on a new scale.[19]

American successes were regular but small-scale, but the final reckoning for Cornwallis's army was not far away and it would be delivered by the Ulster-Americans, who were at the heart of every victory for the infant United States.

On 7 October 1780, the final American triumph came that little bit closer when the battle lines were drawn at King's Mountain in South Carolina. It was here that 900 Ulster-American backwoodsmen gathered under the command of Col. William Campbell and four other colonels who were all Presbyterian elders. Campbell, the son of Ulster emigrants to Virginia, would become a household name throughout the states for the instruction to his men to, "Shout like hell and fight like devils." Numbered among the Ulster-American officers were the McDowell brothers, Joseph and William, the sons of Joseph McDowell who had arrived in America from Ulster in 1730; yet another brother, Charles, also fought in the war.

Campbell's men were outnumbered by almost two to one by the loyalist army under Major Patrick Ferguson but the odds did not

*The Ulster-American backwoodsmen gather for the Battle
of King's Mountain. (Tennessee State Archives)*

intimidate them. In fact, Ferguson was completely outmanoeuvred
and overrun. In the end, he was to be numbered among the 180
British that lost their lives, while about 1,000 loyalists were taken
prisoner by the Ulster-Americans. News of King's Mountain broke
in the *News Letter* of 6–9 February 1781, which carried the following
letter from William Davison to General Sumner:

Camp, Rocky-river, Oct. 12th, 1780

Sir,
    I have the pleasure of handing you very agreeable intelligence
from the West. Ferguson, the great partizan, has miscarried. This
we are assured of by Mr. Tate, Brigade Major in Gen. Sumpter's late
command; the particulars from that gentleman's mouth stand thus:
That Colonels Campbell, Cleveland, Shelby, Seveer, Williams,

The Battle of King's Mountain – an Ulster-American triumph. (Library of Congress)

Brandon, Lacey, &c. formed a conjunct body near Gilbert Town, consisting of 3000. From this body were selected 1600 good horse, who immediately went in pursuit of Col. Ferguson, who was making his way to Charlotte. Our people overtook him posted on King's Mountain, and on the evening of the 7th instant, at four o'clock, began the attack, which continued 47 minutes. Colonel Ferguson fell in the action besides 160 of his men; 810 were made prisoners, including the British; 150 of the prisoners are wounded: 1500 stand of arms fell into our hands. Col. Ferguson had about 1400 men. Our people surrounded them, and the enemy surrendered. We lost about 20 men, among whom is Major Chronicle, of Lincoln country; Col. Williams is mortally wounded. The number of our wounded cannot be ascertained. This blow will certainly affect the British considerably. The Brigade Major who gives this, was in the action. The above is true. The blow is great. I give you joy upon the occasion.

I am, &c.

(signed)   William Davison[20]

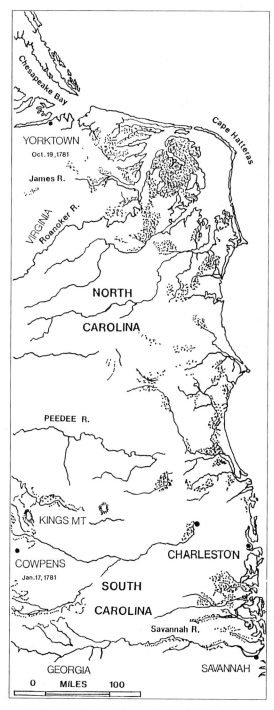

Map 6: *King's Mountain and Cowpens.*

William Campbell was promoted to brigadier-general and received a warm letter of congratulation from Washington for his brilliant victory. King's Mountain was more than just a victory, however, for the whole war now took on a different mantel. Richard Morris set the battle in its proper context:

> The defeat of the Loyalists at King's Mountain destroyed once and for all Tory prestige in North Carolina and forced Cornwallis to retreat south across the state line to Winnsborough.[21]

The British could run but they could not hide! The next blow was to fall on 17 January 1781, at the Battle of Cowpens in South Carolina. Cornwallis had sent Lt. Col. Banastre Tarleton to deal with Dan Morgan's frontiersmen, who again included Major Joseph McDowell among their ranks, but, as at King's Mountain, superiority of numbers was to count for nothing. Morgan, a native of Ballynascreen in County Londonderry, was now about to carve his own place in American history. He had led his Virginia riflemen in many engagements before Cowpens, most notably at Saratoga, but this was to be his masterpiece. Morris describes the scene:

> Morgan's moves were unorthodox, but his strategy made this the patriots' best fought battle of the whole war. The raw militia were placed in the front line. Behind them were the Continentals and some seasoned Virginia militiamen, ordered to hold their ground at all cost. To the rear, in a low ridge sheltered from British fire, Morgan placed his calvary.[22]

As the British advanced Morgan steadied his front line, urging his men to, "Look for the epaulets! Pick off the epaulets!"[23] After two volleys the front rank withdrew to the rear, encouraging Tarleton's men to come on. Morgan now ordered his Virginians to charge with fixed bayonets, followed by the calvary. They simply swept the field, giving no quarter, just as Tarleton would have given none to them.

The Americans could not have wished for a more auspicious start to the new year of 1781. The British had lost 100 men dead, 200 wounded and 500 taken prisoner. Four out of every five men engaged had fallen to the Americans. As well as men, the British were also forced to surrender many valuable supplies. Cowpens

General Dan Morgan. (Culver Pictures)

The Battle of Cowpens – Dan Morgan's masterpiece. (Library of Congress)

was Dan Morgan's crowning moment. In recognition of his achievement, he was awarded a gold medal by Congress and his place in America's hall of fame was secured forever.

Although Morgan was very much the man of the moment, he was not the only Ulster-American rewarded for his part in this great victory. General Andrew Pickens, the son of an Ulster family who had settled in Pennsylvania, was given a sword of honour, while Col. Howard received from Congress a silver medal. Pickens would continue to bite at the heals of Cornwallis as he retreated north for the final act.

And yet Cowpens was a victory that might never have happened, for Morgan, like Col. John Stark in New Hampshire, had earlier resigned his command when he had been passed over for promotion by others whom he considered less deserving. This impatience appears to have been one of the less creditable characteristics shared by Washington's Ulster-American officers. Yet, in the end, they never failed their commander, returning to the

The Battle of Cowpens (Yale University Art Gallery)

colours and, in the case of Stark and Morgan, making the British pay for their bad temper. Morgan was undoubtedly motivated to avenge a beating he had once received at the hands of an English officer. He could never have anticipated how sweet that revenge would be.

Just nine months later, on 19 October 1781, General Cornwallis surrendered his army to General George Washington at Yorktown, Virginia. The British had been drawn north in an attempt to engage the forces of General Nathaniel Greene, but by the time he reached Virginia, Cornwallis was so weakened by the loss of men and supplies that he had no option but to make camp and await evacuation by the Royal Navy. At the same time, Washington withdrew his forces, which were concentrating for an attack on New York and moved them to Yorktown, supported by 6,700 French troops under the Comte de Rochambeau. At the same time, a French naval squadron under Admiral de Grasse, blockaded Chesapeke Bay, ending any hopes of a relief mission by the Royal Navy.

Cornwallis was completely surrounded.

In offering unconditional surrender, Cornwallis offered America final victory, but more importantly her freedom. Everyone knew this was the case; even the British parliament, where Lord North's government now fell and was succeeded by the Whigs under Rockingham and Shelburne. It would take almost two more years before the British would formally recognise the independence of the United States, in the Treaty of Paris signed on 3 September 1783, but it was worth waiting. As well as recognising the new nation, the British government also conceded important fishing rights to the Americans in Canadian waters and accepted extensive boundaries, marked by the Great Lakes in the north and the Mississippi river in the west. Apart from independence itself, this territorial agreement was America's most significant gain in the treaty, bearing testimony to the skilful representation of their case by Benjamin Franklin, John Adams and John Jay.

In November 1783, George Washington led his victorious army through the streets of New York, which at last had been evacuated by the British. On 4 December, at Fraunces Tavern, he bade an emotional farewell to the officers who had served him so well. Henry Knox, as we have said, was the first to receive this honour, but he was only one of many.

There are more names to add to the list of the Ulster-American officers already referred to: Brigadier-General John Armstrong who was born in Ulster and settled in the Cumberland Valley in Pennsylvania – a prominent figure in frontier fights with the Indians, where he first met and became friends with George Washington under whom he fought, commanding Pennsylvania troops at the battles of Brandywine and Germantown (Armstrong's son, John Jr, rose to the rank of adjutant-general and, like Henry Knox, later became Secretary of War); General Ephriam Blaine was born in Donegal and became Washington's quarter-master; General John Clark was a native of Antrim; Generals James Ewing and William Henry were both descended from Ulster immigrants; General Irvine was born in Enniskillen and raised the sixth Pennsylvania regiment in the war; General Andrew Lewis, a native of Donegal, was at one stage in the running for the post of commander-in-chief; General William Maxwell came form Ulster; General James Miller was born in New Londonderry; General Thomas Polk was of Ulster descent; Generals Enoch Poor and

The final victory – the American flag is planted in triumph over
the battlefield at Yorktown. (National Park Service, Yorktown)

Francis Preston were both sons of Ulster families; General Thomas
Robinson and General Rutherford were of Ulster descent; General
Walter Stewart was born in Londonderry and General William
Thompson was born in Maghera, the brother of Charles Thompson,
the man who first transcribed the Declaration of Independence.

To this list of fighting men, should also be added the names of
those Ulster-Americans who supported America's cause with their
worldly goods. Chief among this number are Blair McClenaghan, a
native of Ulster who gave $50,000; James Mease and his uncle, John
Mease, from Strabane, who gave $25,000 and $20,000 respectively;
John Dunlop, also from Strabane, also contributed $20,000; John
Murray from Belfast gave $30,000; John Donaldson form
Dungannon gave $10,000; finally, Thomas Barkley, John Nesbit and
John Nixon, who were all descended from Ulster families, each put
$30,000 into the coffers of the United States.

As one pictures the Stars and Stripes fluttering proudly over the
battlefield at Yorktown, the words of W. F. Marshall ring loud and
clear and true:

There is no other race in the United States that can produce a Roll of Honour so long and so shining with distinction. Add to it the colonels and majors and captains of this race, the sergeants, riflemen, troopers and gunners, add to it the Ulster-Irish in the Navy, and who shall deny our claim to have done more, much more than any others to make the United States?[24]

EPILOGUE

IT is significant that the grave of the unknown soldier of the War of Independence should be placed in the graveyard of the Presbyterian meeting house in Alexandria, Virginia. During the American bicentennial celebrations, in 1976, the Bushmills-born journalist, John Speers of New Jersey, paid tribute to Ulster's part in the American revolution:

> There in soil literally heavy with Ulster dust, lie men from Antrim, Armagh, Derry, Donegal, Down, Fermanagh and Tyrone, their names and lives remembered only in stone, their deeds and achievements saluted by the miniature American flags which flutter perpetually over the last resting place of every known Revolutionary War soldier.[1]

Yet America's War of Independence was only the end of a new beginning. Great destiny beckoned America and it was a destiny in which the Ulster-American people would play a leading role, just as they had done in the war which made that future possible.

Beginning with the creation of the Constitution, Ulster men and women were to the fore in the development of every aspect of American life. Indeed, the Ulster-Scots became, in many ways, the archetypal American – God-fearing, anxious to better themselves and always prepared to fight for their beliefs, in both war and politics.

The American frontier moved west in the wake of pioneers from the Ulster-American community, like Daniel Boone and Davy Crockett. American literature was enriched by the contributions of the likes of Edgar Alan Poe, while men of Ulster descent like

Thomas Mellon and John D. Rockefeller, became giants in American commercial life. During the American Civil War, the finest generals produced on both sides could claim Ulster ancestry, namely Stonewall Jackson in the South and Ulysses S. Grant in the North. At the very pinnacle of the Ulster-American achievement stood eleven men who became President of the United States and provided America with, arguably, two of her greatest chief executives in Andrew Jackson and Woodrow Wilson. The record reaches right up to the present day, for in 1969, the first man to set foot on the moon, Neil Armstrong, was descended from a County Fermanagh family.

The Ulster-American connection is a heritage that is long and rich. It has blossomed and flourished as the United States have grown from those thirteen original states to its place today as the greatest power on earth. But the roots of this mighty tree reach deeper that those early colonies, for the very source of its nourishment lies in the counties of Ulster which gave of her best in the early years of the eighteenth century and gave it to the land that would make men free, just as that land was given its freedom by the sons and daughters of Ulster.

NOTES

Full references to the works quoted are contained in the bibliography.

I   THE ULSTER HOMELAND

1. Stewart, *The Narrow Ground*, p. 39.
2. ibid. p. 39.
3. Leyburn, *The Scotch-Irish*, p. 139.
4. Allen, *To Ulster's Credit*, p. 22.
5. Leyburn, pp. 142–3.
6. Roosevelt, *Stories Of The Great West*, pp. 16–17.
7. Leyburn, p. 162.

II   THE NEW WORLD

1. Brogan, *History of United States of America*, p. 50.

III   ULSTER SAILS WEST

1. *Belfast News Letter*, 1774.
2. Marshall, *Ulster Sails West*, pp. 12–13.
3. ibid. p. 16.
4. Leyburn, p. 171.
5. *Belfast News Letter*, 29 June 1750.
6. ibid. 6 June 1752.
7. ibid. 21 April 1767.
8. ibid. 20 February 1767.
9. Roosevelt, p. 16.
10. Marshall, p. 26.
11. Roosevelt, p. 17.

IV   CROWN AND COLONY

1. *Belfast News Letter*, 24 September 1771.
2. ibid. 20–24 January 1775.
3. Commager, *The War of Independence*, p. 98.
4. *Belfast News Letter*, 30 January 1770.
5. ibid. 6 July 1770.
6. ibid. 7 August 1770.
7. ibid. 20 August 1771.
8. ibid. 27 August 1771.
9. Allen, p. 41–2.
10. Marshall, p. 28.
11. *Belfast News Letter*, 28 January – 1 February 1774.
12. ibid. 13–17 January 1775.
13. ibid. 16 March 1773.
14. ibid. 20–24 August 1773.
15. ibid. 24–27 August 1773.
16. ibid. 19 April 1774.

V   THE PEN AND THE SWORD

1. *Belfast News Letter*, 23–27 June 1775.
2. ibid. 21–25 July 1775.
3. ibid. 18–21 July 1775.
4. ibid. 11–15 May 1775.
5. ibid. 8 April 1778.
6. ibid. 26–29 May 1778.
7. ibid. 8–12 September 1775.
8. Morris, *The Making of a Nation*, p. 11.
9. *Belfast New Letter*, 25–29 August 1775.
10. Marshall, p. 29.
11. Ford, *The Scotch-Irish in America*, p. 512.
12. Commager, p. 128.
13. *Belfast News Letter*, 6–10 September 1776.
14. Brogan, p. 182.

VI   FREE AT LAST

1. Commager, p. 32.
2. *Belfast News Letter*, 18–22 March 1776.
3. Morris, p. 14.
4. ibid. p. 16.
5. ibid. p. 71.

6. *Belfast News Letter*, 28–31 October 1777.
7. Marshall, p. 36.
8. Commager, p. 31.
9. *Belfast News Letter*, 5–9 December 1777.
10. Commager, p. 107.
11. Morris, p. 66.
12. Marshall, p. 30.
13. ibid. p. 31.
14. Ford, p. 518.
15. *Belfast News Letter*, 27–30 October 1778.
16. ibid. 2–6 April 1779.
17. ibid. 12–15 May 1778.
18. ibid. 5–8 October 1778.
19. Commager, p. 120.
20. *Belfast News Letter*, 6–9 February 1781.
21. Morris, p. 83.
22. ibid. p. 83.
23. ibid. p. 83.
24. Marshall, pp. 38–9.

EPILOGUE

1. Allen, p. 61.

BIBLIOGRAPHY

NEWSPAPERS:

Belfast News Letter, 1737–82.

BOOKS:

Allen, Sam, *To Ulster's Credit*, N.P.,N.D.

Brogan, Hugh, *Longman History Of The United States Of America*, Longman, 1985.

Commager, Henry Steele, et al, *A New World to Conquer* (Volume 1 of *The American Destiny*), Orbis, 1986.

Commager, Henry Steele, et al, *The War of Independence* (Volume 2 of *The American Destiny*), Orbis, 1986.

Dickson, R. J., *Ulster Emigration To Colonial America, 1718–1775*, Routledge And Kegan Paul, 1966.

Fitzpatrick, Rory, *God's Frontiersmen: The Scots-Irish Epic*, Weidenfeld and Nicholson, 1989.

Ford, Henry Jones, *The Scotch-Irish In America*, Princeton University Press, 1915.

Leyburn, J. G., *The Scotch-Irish: A Social History*, The University of North Carolina Press, 1962.

Marker, Sherry, *Illustrated History of the United States*, Brompton Books, 1988.

Marshall, W. F., *Ulster Sails West*, N.P., 1943.

Morris, Richard B., *The Making of a Nation* (Volume 2 of *The LIFE History of the United States*), Time, 1963.

Patterson, Samuel C., Roger H. Davidson & Randall B. Ripley, *A More Perfect Union: Introduction to American Government*, Dorsey Press, 1982.

Roosevelt, Theodore, *Stories Of The Great West*, Appleton Century Crofts, 1888.

Stewart, A. T. Q., *The Narrow Ground: Aspects of Ulster, 1609–1969*, Faber & Faber, 1977.

INDEX

Numbers in *italics* indicate an illustration of the subject.

ULSTER SOCIETY PUBLICATIONS

THE ORANGE LARK and Other Songs of the Orange Tradition
148mm x 210mm•96pp•£2.00

LILLIBURLERO and More Songs of the Orange Tradition
148mm x 210mm•108pp•£2.00

THE HIGHEST CALL: Ulster and the American Presidency
By Ronnie Hanna . . . 210mm x 297mm•40pp•£3.00

FOR ULSTER & HER FREEDOM: the Story of the April 1914 Gunrunning
By David Hume . . . 210mm x 297mm•48pp•£3.00

IRELAND'S PHYSICAL FORCE TRADITION TODAY: Reflections on the
Enniskillen Massacre – By Clifford Smyth . . . 210mm x 297mm•38pp•£3.00

COVENANT & CHALLENGE: Reflections on Ulster's Identity
By Revd. Brett Ingram . . . 148mm x 210mm•146pp•£4.95

THE ULSTER COVENANT: Pictorial History of the 1912 Home Rule Crisis
Edited by Gordon Lucy . . . 210mm x 200mm•100pp•£5.95

LORD MACAULAY ON LONDONDERRY, AUGHRIM, ENNISKILLEN
& THE BOYNE – Edited by Gordon Lucy . . . 148mm x 210mm•94pp•£3.00

LIFE-LINE TO FREEDOM: Ulster in the Second World War
By Derrick Gibson-Harries . . . 148mm x 210mm•128pp•£4.50

WILLIAM JOHNSTON OF BALLYKILBEG
By Aiken McClelland . . . 153mm x 235mm•160pp•£5.50

"PARDON ME BOY": The Americans in Ulster 1942-45 — A Pictorial
Record – Edited by Ronnie Hanna . . . 210mm x 200mm•100pp•£5.95

NEVER CALL RETREAT: The Life and Times of Ulysses S. Grant, Ulster-
American Hero – By Ronnie Hanna . . . 153mm x 235mm•160pp•£5.95

THE FOUNDATION OF NORTHERN IRELAND
By David Trimble MP . . . 148mm x 210mm•48pp•£1.00

THE EASTER REBELLION OF 1916
David Trimble MP . . . 148mm x 210mm•44pp•£1.00

THE ULSTER SOCIETY

THE Society was established in June 1985 with the aim of promoting and preserving Ulster-British heritage. The rich culture of Ulster is reflected in the work we do.

Although our headquarters is in Banbridge, the Society's Publications and Membership departments are based in Brownlow House, Lurgan, and our activities cover the whole of Ulster. We have members and corporate members in every major town as well as in England, Scotland and Wales. Events have been held in all areas.

Ulster's contribution to the growth and development of other countries is reflected in the presence of members in the USA, Canada, Australia and South Africa.

JOIN THE ULSTER SOCIETY

THE work The Ulster Society is doing is vital to the future of our country and it is work that must be continued if we are to survive. To carry out that work effectively we need your support. Membership of the Society will entitle you to notification of all our events and a free copy of each issue of *New Ulster* as it is published. You will also be encouraged to take part in the promotion of various projects in which we are involved.

I trust that you will give this appeal your sympathetic consideration and look forward to welcoming you as a member in the near future.

The membership fee is £10.00 p.a. (£5.00 for OAPs, Students and Unemployed). Please return your remittance to . . .

The Membership Secretary
The Ulster Society
Brownlow House
Windsor Avenue
Lurgan
Co. Armagh BT67 9BJ